EARLY YEARS ACTIVITY CHEST

Number activities

British Library Cataloguing-in-Publication Data
A catalogue record for this book is available from the British Library.

ISBN 0 439 01730 0

ACKNOWLEDGEMENTS
The publishers gratefully acknowledge permission to reproduce the following copyright material:

Karen King for 'The birthday party' © 2000, Karen King; Celia Warren for 'At the supermarket' © 2000, Celia Warren; Ann Bryant for 'Ten little skittles' © 2000, Ann Bryant. All previously unpublished.

Every effort has been made to trace copyright holders and the publishers apologize for any inadvertent omission.

AUTHOR
Lisa Bessinger

EDITOR
Clare Miller

ASSISTANT EDITOR
Lesley Sudlow

SERIES DESIGNER
Lynne Joesbury

DESIGNER
Clare Brewer

ILLUSTRATIONS
Maureen Galvani

COVER PHOTOGRAPH
Fiona Pragoff

In loving memory of my baby nephew, Jarrod

Text © 2000 Lisa Bessinger
© 2000 Scholastic Ltd

Designed using Adobe Pagemaker
Published by Scholastic Ltd, Villiers House,
Clarendon Avenue, Leamington Spa, Warwickshire CV32 5PR

Visit our website at scholastic.co.uk

1 2 3 4 5 6 7 8 9 0   0 1 2 3 4 5 6 7 8 9

CONTENTS

CONTENTS

Introduction

The aims of the series

This book is one of a series that provides the early years practitioner with a range of hands-on activities covering all six areas of learning encompassed in the Early Learning Goals for pre-school children. *Number Activities* includes 48 main activity ideas in an easy-to-use format and 24 photocopiable sheets, all of which are aimed at four-year-olds with support and extension for children aged between three and five years of age.

In everyday life we come across numbers that quantify things such as our age, weight, time, date and the price of something. Children have a natural fascination for numbers and become aware of them at a very early age. How many times have you heard children saying that someone else has more sweets than him or her, and then counting to see if they are right in their assumption? On the other hand, many adults who have had bad experiences with maths tend to avoid anything to do with numbers. This book hopes to move away from this fear of numbers and aims to show that maths can be a fun and enjoyable experience for both adults and children alike.

Children are encouraged to use maths in practical and fun ways, helping them to see it as functional, non-threatening and relevant to them. The activities here provide lots of opportunities to discuss ideas and to begin to use the kind of vocabulary inherent to basic mathematical concepts.

The book is packed full of activities that will inspire children and provide ample meaningful opportunities to explore and discover the wonderful and exciting world of numbers and how they are used all around us. It will help children to recognize the number sequence 0 to 10, to put a name to each numeral, to gain pleasure and confidence in using numbers and begin to understand what they represent.

How to use this book

This book is divided into six chapters covering Personal, social and emotional development, Communication, language and literacy, Mathematical development, Knowledge and understanding of the world, Physical development and Creative development. Each chapter contains eight activities, which cover a wide spectrum of ideas providing a well-balanced curriculum. At the beginning of each activity there is a section outlining the key 'Learning objectives' that the activities provide in terms of the area of learning covered by that chapter.

The range of activities can be adapted to suit the individual needs and abilities of the children in your care. The aim of this book is not to teach children to count to ten by rote, but to provide a wide selection of stimulating activities which will help them to understand and develop number concepts through active participation. If there is an activity which seems to have particular appeal for children, repeat or adapt this activity to reinforce the skills they have learnt. It is also important to use every available opportunity within the daily programme to initiate discussion on number concepts; for example when a child is doing a puzzle talk about how many pieces they have put in, how many are left on the table and so on. Some of the activities are for the whole group's participation, such as 'Nature collage' on page 49 in Chapter 6, whereas others such as 'Shopping spree' on page 34 in Chapter 4, concentrate on small groups of children.

Some of the activities require a minimum amount of preparation such as 'Walk the number line' on page 44 in Chapter 5, however others require more such as 'Crack the safe' on page 22 in Chapter 2. The children can help with some of the preparation such as in 'Phone a friend' on page 12 in Chapter 1, and in other cases preparation can be reduced by using number cards for more than one activity such as in 'Fishing game' on page 26 and 'Bags of numbers' on page 27 in Chapter 3.

The 'What to do' section of each activity provides step-by-step instructions on carrying out the activity, ensuring that children are encouraged to participate, and that the material is relevant and stimulating for them. For each activity, there are suggestions on how to simplify and extend the main idea depending on the abilities and age of the children in the group.

Using the photocopiable sheets

Many of the activities are supported by photocopiable activity sheets, which are used in different ways. There are worksheets dealing with numbers for the children to complete such as 'Here comes the post' on page 40 in Chapter 4, while others contain useful recipes such as 'Puffy paint number pictures' on page 50 in Chapter 6, or multicultural ideas such as 'Fruit salad' on page 11 in Chapter 1. Finally, there are a number of general photocopiable sheets all linked to specific activities in the book.

Resources

Pre-school children learn best through hands-on activities, talking, active participation, repetition, asking questions and solving problems all of which require concrete experiences. The activities in this book make use of a wide variety of different resources, all of which are readily available in most pre-school environments, from books, collage materials, role-play materials and manipulative equipment, to natural objects such as those used in 'Nature collage' on page 49 in Chapter 6. Some of the other activities encourage children to choose their own materials such as 'Colourful mosaics' on page 54 in Chapter 6, thereby providing them with the opportunity of freedom of choice. Children need concrete experiences in order to manipulate and arrange the materials and information at their disposal and in so doing, make sense of the world around them.

Links with home

The connection between home and the group is a vital one and parents and carers need to be actively involved in ensuring the continuity of their children's education. To strengthen this link, each of the activities contains a practical suggestion that can be followed through at home. Use these ideas to show parents and carers how much fun can be gained from numbers, and to encourage a positive attitude to the subject. For the purpose of this book, parents and carers should be encouraged to draw their child's attention to numbers in their immediate environment by counting cars in the street or items bought in the supermarket, looking at house numbers and so on, with their children.

Multicultural links

Many of the activities provide a multicultural activity idea, which will help children to recognize that there are many different cultures and religions in the world around us, and that they all have different celebrations and festivals. The main aim is to encourage children to respect, be tolerant of and sensitive to the individual differences and cultural and religious backgrounds of others.

In conclusion, encourage each child's desire to learn more and help them find pleasure in what they do, but most of all encourage them to have fun! Providing new, exciting and stimulating activities helps each child to understand and give meaning to number concepts. They will slowly begin to realize that adding another object to a group represents a higher number in the numerical scale, and that removing one results in a lower number. This realization will not happen automatically but will take place over a period of time. Letting children enjoy what they are doing helps them develop a positive attitude towards learning and provides a stable foundation on which to base future learning experiences.

This chapter provides a range of opportunities for children to express themselves and to think about the needs and beliefs of others. The activities encourage children to collaborate with others and include role-playing phoning a friend and playing a group building game.

Personal, social and emotional development

GROUP SIZE
Four children.

TIMING
20 to 25 minutes.

HOME LINKS
Ask parents and carers to invite their children to think of ways that they can help with chores around the house.

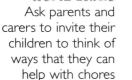

MULTICULTURAL LINKS
Show the children pictures of hand decorations known as mehndi in India, and urge them to decorate their handprints in a similar manner by drawing interesting patterns on them using finger-paint.

HELPING HANDS

Learning objective
To have a developing awareness of the needs of others.

What you need
A3 sheets of coloured card; A3 sheets of skin-coloured paper in a variety of shades; scissors; old magazines; glue; spreaders; a marker pen.

What to do
Invite four children to sit with you at the table and ask them if they can think of different ways in which they have helped other people. Discuss the different things that they can do to help others and lead them to think about which parts of the body are very useful in carrying out tasks. Hold up your hands and ask them to tell you how many hands we have. When the children have answered, put one hand down and ask if they can now tell you how many fingers we have on each hand. Count the fingers on your hand out loud, touching each finger as you count. Repeat with your other hand before asking the children if anyone knows how many fingers that makes in total.

Next, ask each child to choose a piece of skin-coloured paper that is closest to their own and to trace around their hands. Cut out the outlines and stick these to the top section of an A3 sheet of card. Clearly label each set of handprints with the child's name and number each finger, one to five, from left to right. Once this is done, ask the children to look through old magazines for pictures of ways in which we help other people, such as taking a dog for a walk. Cut out these pictures and display them underneath the handprints with a written description under each picture. Display all the 'helping hand' pictures on the display board under a large heading entitled 'Our helping hands.'

Dan

Taking a dog for a walk

Support
Younger children will need help tracing around their hands.

Extension
Encourage the children to number their own fingers on their handprints.

GROUP SIZE
Four children.

TIMING
15 to 20 minutes.

PINKIE PIG GAME

Learning objectives

To work as part of a group, taking turns and sharing fairly; to select resources independently.

What you need

Eight pieces of pink card; dice; coloured spot stickers; scissors; sticky-backed plastic; the photocopiable sheet on page 61; a large envelope.

Preparation

Copy the photocopiable sheet onto eight pieces of pink card. Stick coloured spots onto each of the black spots on the pig template. Cover four of the cards with sticky-backed plastic to make baseboards. Cut the second set of cards carefully along the marked lines. Place both sets of cards in a large envelope until required.

HOME LINKS
Invite parents and carers to take the 'Pinkie pig game' home overnight to play with their children.

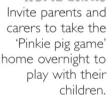

What to do

Give each of the four children a baseboard and place the loose pig pieces face upward in the centre of the table. Emphasize to the children that they must play the game in a clockwise direction. Each player takes a turn to roll the dice and to count out loud the number of spots when it stops. The first player to roll a '1' starts the game by picking up a matching card piece with one spot on it from among the pieces in the centre of the table. Place this card over the correct section on the pig outline on the baseboard. If the child rolls the dice and already has the matching piece then he misses a turn and the next child takes a turn. The first player to complete their pig is the winner, but the game continues until all cards are complete.

At the end of the activity, show the children that when all the pieces are placed on the baseboard they make up a whole image.

MULTICULTURAL LINKS
Make a board game of people wearing traditional costumes of various different cultures, using the photocopiable sheet on page 62, and play in the same way as the 'Pinkie pig game' – the aim being to match the different people to those on their individual baseboard.

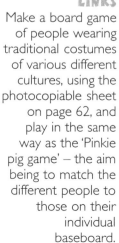

Support

Younger children will require close supervision when playing this game as they may need help counting the number of spots on the dice and playing pieces.

Extension

Extend the game for older children by placing a number symbol instead of a spot on the baseboard. Ask them to match the number of dots to the number symbol. Encourage the children to make their own board pieces.

GROUP SIZE
Four children.

TIMING
20 minutes.

HOME LINKS
Explain to parents
and carers what you
have been doing
and provide them
with a picture recipe
for the preparation
of a green salad,
which they can
make with their
children at home.

**MULTICULTURAL
ACTIVITIES**
Make the sweet,
barfi, which is given
as a present during
the Hindu festival of
Divali. (See the
recipe on the
photocopiable sheet
on page 64.)
NB Check for any
allergies and dietary
requirements.

FRUIT SALAD

Learning objectives
To work together as part of a group to make a
fruit salad; to count, compare and record the
number of ingredients used on a pictorial chart.

What you need
A selection of fresh fruit; chopping boards; bowl;
fruit knives; aprons; basket; kitchen roll; one picture
of each fruit to be used; A3 sheet of paper; glue; spreaders; juicer; coloured
pencils; marker pen; the photocopiable sheet on page 63.

Preparation
Ensure that all the ingredients are collected beforehand and that all the
utensils required are laid out on a table. Make a pictorial chart on an A3
sheet of paper by writing, 'Fruit used in our fruit salad' at the top of the
paper and the numbers 1 to 10 down the left-hand side. Stick a picture of
each fruit to be used along the bottom of the page.

What to do
At the start of the activity, help each child to put on an apron and ask
them to wash their hands. Each child then chooses two pieces of fruit
from among those in the basket on the table. Let the children wash the
fruit then dry it on kitchen roll. Ask the children to peel fruit such as
satsumas and bananas. Do any peeling yourself that requires using a
knife, then closely supervise the children in slicing the fruit. Introduce
the children to the mathematical concept of sequencing by saying, 'First
we are going to wash the fruit, then we will cut it up and lastly we will eat
what we have made.' **NB** Check for any allergies and dietary requirements.

Encourage the children to talk about and compare the difference in
texture, shape, colour, size, aroma and outer covering of the fruits while
they prepare them. Stimulate discussion by asking questions such as,
'How many pips can you count in the apple that you are preparing?'.

When the children have finished
preparing the fruit, place it all in a bowl
to be eaten during snack time. Squeeze
juice from a number of oranges and pour
over the completed fruit salad. Once all
the fruit salad utensils have been cleared
away, ask each child to mark on the chart
what fruit they added to the fruit salad
using coloured pencils. Finish by giving
each child a copy of the photocopiable
sheet on page 63 for them to complete.

Support
Younger children can help squeeze
oranges and pour the juice over the fruit
salad rather than cutting up the fruit.

Extension
Prepare a large picture recipe chart for
the children to follow.

GROUP SIZE
Two children.

TIMING
20 minutes.

PHONE A FRIEND

Learning objectives

To consider the consequences of their words for themselves and others; to be confident to try new activities and speak in a familiar group.

What you need

Two old touch-tone telephones; old telephone directories; play money; large cardboard box; red paint; paintbrushes; sheets of paper; marker pen; shoebox; craft knife; two small chairs; two small tables; the photocopiable sheet on page 65.

Preparation

Make a telephone booth by cutting one end off a cardboard box that is large enough for a child to stand up in. Make a hole for the window in one side of the box and cut down the right-hand edge of this side so that it opens like a door. Help the children to paint the box red. Once dry, place the box in the role-play corner and put one chair, table, telephone directory and telephone inside. Cut a slot for coins in the lid of a shoebox and place alongside the telephone in the telephone box. The other table, chair, telephone and telephone directory should be set up within hearing distance of the telephone box.

What to do

Show the children the telephone box and the other telephone urging them to take turns making 'calls' to each other. Explain that when we speak to people on the telephone, we should not shout at them or slam the phone down as this is very rude and we would not like someone to do the same to us. Show them how to use the telephone directories in case they need to look a number up.

Tell the children that when we make a phone call from a telephone box, we need to put money in a box in order to pay the telephone company for the call. Show them how to place the plastic coins in the hole in the top of the shoebox to pay for the calls that they make. Encourage the children to role-play how they answer and talk on the telephone, asking the child in the telephone box to call the other child. Invite the children to take 'messages' for each other using the pen and sheets of paper.

Provide the children with copies of the photocopiable sheet on page 65 to colour and complete.

Support

Younger children will enjoy having 'conversations' on their own.

Extension

Encourage the children to find out what their home phone number is and ask someone to write it down for them, or better still, do it themselves, and then see if they are able to dial the number in the correct sequence on a play telephone.

HOME LINKS
Ask parents and carers to show their children how they look up telephone numbers in their phone books when they need to make a call to a specific person. Encourage them to teach their children how to answer the telephone in the correct manner.

THREE LITTLE PIGS

Learning objectives

To be confident to speak in a familiar group; to select resources independently.

What you need

The story of 'The Three Little Pigs' (Traditional); straw; sticks; plastic bricks; four strips of cardboard long enough to fit around a child's head; pink and brown card; scissors; stapler; boxes; pencil.

Preparation

Cut out six ears from the pink card and two larger ones from the brown card before stapling two to each of the four strips of card. Place the straw, sticks, ears and bricks into separate boxes.

What to do

Read the story of 'The Three Little Pigs' to the children the day before you carry out the activity so that they are all familiar with it. Ensure that you have a large enough area allocated for this activity so that the children have sufficient space to move freely and safely. Most of the children will welcome the opportunity of acting out the story, but some will not be ready for this activity and should not be forced to participate. Allow these children just to observe.

Show the children taking part the boxes containing the various props at their disposal, and help them to decide who is going to play what part in the story. Invite the children to act out their version of the story, making up their own words as they go along. Encourage the children to change their voice when they play the 'wolf' or one of the 'pigs', for added effect. Some of the children will remember exact sections of the story such as, 'Little pig, little pig, let me come in' and should be encouraged to repeat them if they wish to.

Support

Read the story to the children a number of times in order that they become familiar with it.

Extension

Invite older children to act out their version of the story for the other children or for some of the parents and carers.

GROUP SIZE
Three children.

TIMING
15 to 20 minutes.

NUMBER COLLAGE

Learning objective
To select and use resources independently.

What you need
Cardboard templates of numbers 1 to 5 in different sizes; fabric remnants; coloured paper; wallpaper and foil scraps; sandpaper and any other suitable collage materials; scissors; glue; spreaders; A3 sheets of coloured card; five empty margarine tubs; five sticky labels; marker pen.

Preparation
Using the card templates cut out a collection of different number shapes from the fabric, wallpaper scraps and so on, making sure that you have a variety of different size numbers cut from different materials.

Write a number from 1 to 5 on each of the sticky labels, and attach one to each of the margarine tubs before placing the tubs in their correct numerical order on the table.

What to do
Invite the children to come to the table and to create a picture using any of the materials displayed. Stress that the position and choice of numbers used is completely up to them.

Encourage each child to talk about the numbers that they choose for their picture and while they are working, invite them to talk about the different materials offered such as their texture, size and so on. Ask each child how old they are and encourage them to look in the tubs for a number that is the same as their age. Explain that every picture will be unique, as everyone is an individual and therefore will choose different things.

Support
Start by offering collage numbers 1 to 3.

Extension
Increase the number of collage numbers to 1 to 10, with the children making the numbered sticky labels for the margarine tubs.

HOME LINKS
Ask parents and carers to allow their children to choose what clothes they want to wear the next day.

MULTICULTURAL LINKS
Make a similar picture by collaging numerals from the number systems of different cultures.

GROUP SIZE
Four children.

TIMING
20 minutes.

HOME LINKS
Ask parents and carers to draw their children's attention to the different types of buildings in their immediate environment. Point out that a big house needs more bricks to build it than a smaller one.

BUILDING FUN

Learning objective

To work as part of a group, taking turns and sharing fairly, understanding that there needs to be agreed codes of behaviour to work together harmoniously.

What you need

A collection of building blocks; small screen; large cotton reels; kitchen-roll tubes; lids of boxes; pieces of card; marker pen; boxes in a variety of sizes; plastic animals and people; two baskets.

Preparation

Ensure that you have sufficient building blocks for two groups of two children to have at least ten blocks each. Place the building accessories – cotton reels, lids of boxes, and so on – in two baskets alongside the blocks and clear a space that will be big enough for both groups to work in. Divide the work area in two with a small screen.

What to do

Invite two children to come with you to the block area and to count out ten blocks between them that they want to use for their structure. Encourage the children to touch each block as they count, with both children agreeing that they have ten blocks in total. Repeat the same with another two children. Ask each pair to place their set of blocks on one side of the screen, so that they cannot see what the other pair are doing, and hand each pair one of the baskets of accessories. Ask both pairs to build a structure using the blocks and accessories provided. As the children work, talk to them about what they are doing, how many blocks they have used, still have to use and so on. Help the children to develop mathematical concepts by using language for size such as 'tall' and 'narrow', and encourage them to think about the position of numbers by asking questions such as, 'How many blocks are 'on top of', 'underneath', block number three, block number four?' and so on. When the structures are complete, display cards with them saying, 'This was made using ten blocks by (name of child) and (name of child)'.

When both pairs have finished, remove the screen from between them and gather the other children together. Ask the children to talk about the structures and how they are both different. Explain that even though both structures were made using ten blocks, they are not the same because people do things differently. Children should then dismantle their structures and another four children take a turn. If you have sufficient space and blocks, leave the structures on display for parents and carers to see.

Support

Provide younger children with just blocks and introduce the building accessories at a later date.

Extension

Ask older children to help make a group project of a town or street using a set amount of blocks.

GROUP SIZE
Four children.

TIMING
15 to 20 minutes.

DREIDEL GAME

Learning objectives
To be confident to try new activities; to understand that people have different cultures that need to be treated with respect.

What you need
Square wooden block; 40 buttons; plastic bowl; permanent marker pen; four small bowls.

Preparation
Make a dreidel from a medium-sized, square, wooden block by writing one each of the following letters on four sides of the block: N, G, H and S. Place ten buttons in each of the four small bowls around the table and put the plastic bowl in the centre.

What to do
Explain to the children that they are going to play a game that is played by Jewish children during Hanukkah. The four Hebrew letters on the sides stand for the words, Nun, Gimel, Hey and Shin, which mean 'A great miracle happened here'. When playing the game, the letters mean the following:

N = Nothing. (You do not get anything from the bowl.)
G = All. (You get all the buttons in the bowl. The other players then add two buttons each to the bowl.)
H = Half. (You get half of the buttons in the bowl.)
S = Put in. (You must add two buttons to the bowl.)

Ask each child to count the number of buttons in their bowl, making sure that they have ten. Start the game by asking each player to place two of their buttons in the bowl in the centre of the table. Each child takes a turn to spin the 'dreidel' to see which side lands facing up. If one of the blank sides faces up, then the player misses a turn and the next player takes a turn. The winner is the player who ends up with all the buttons.

Support
Younger children will need constant adult supervision.

Extension
Encourage older children to make their own dreidels.

HOME LINKS
Write simple instructions for the game and let the children take turns in taking the dreidel game home to play with their parents and carers.

This chapter encourages children to enjoy using and exploring spoken and written language. Activities include making a diary recording dates and news, singing a counting song and discussing the numbered steps of an experiment.

Communication, language and literacy

NUMBER DOMINOES

Learning objective
To read a range of familiar and common words independently.

What you need
A4 sheet of white paper; scissors; sticky-backed plastic; the photocopiable sheet on page 66; a large envelope.

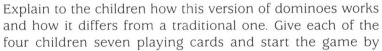

Preparation
Copy the dominoes template on the photocopiable sheet on page 66 onto a piece of card. Cover the card with sticky-backed plastic and cut out the individual cards before placing them into an envelope.

What to do
Explain to the children how this version of dominoes works and how it differs from a traditional one. Give each of the four children seven playing cards and start the game by placing the blank card in the centre of the table. The first child looks to see if he has a blank space on any of his cards that will match either half of the card on the table. If he does have a matching card then he must place that card next to the other one with matching blanks lined up. Each time a card is placed on the table, ask the children to tell you which two numbers are displayed. If a child does not have a matching card, then he misses a turn and the next child plays. The game continues in this manner until all the cards have been placed in their correct position.

During the course of the game, draw the children's attention to the written word and number symbol and encourage them to read the numbers. The player who finishes all his cards first is the winner.

Support
Cut the cards in half and use them to play 'Snap'.

Extension
Encourage older children to make a set of dominoes with an unusual theme, for example draw an animal outline on each rectangle shape and number the various sections.

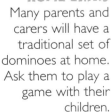

PEEK-A-BOO PICTURES

Learning objective
To use talk to organize, sequence and clarify thinking and ideas.

What you need
Four A4 sheets of coloured card; old household, toy and general interest magazines; scissors; glue; spreaders; tracing paper; craft knife; marker pen; pencil; paper clips; display board.

Preparation
Select two A4-size pictures from the magazines showing things that will be familiar to the children, such as a cat or a dog. Cut them out and stick each one onto a piece of card. When the glue is dry, cover each picture with a sheet of tracing paper and identify six key features on each picture by marking them with a cross. Remove the paper and place on top of a second sheet of card, press down firmly with a pencil and transfer the cross shape to the card. Take off the tracing paper and where the crosses are, draw either a rectangle or a square shape. Using a craft knife, carefully cut three sides of each shape, leaving the fourth side of each one uncut. When this is done, number each 'window' from one to six with a numeral and a written word. Fasten this card over the main picture with paper clips and attach the two completed 'peek-a-boo pictures' to a display board.

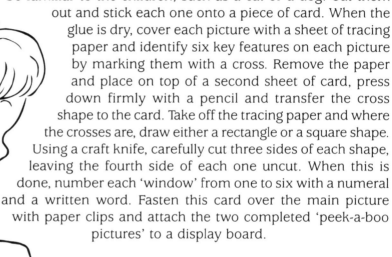

What to do
Tell the children that underneath each numbered flap, a small part of a picture will be revealed, and that they must try to identify the whole picture that it forms part of. Invite each child to take a turn to come up to the board and carefully open one of the flaps, stressing that each flap must be opened in the correct numerical order. Ask each child to tell you the number of the flap that they have just opened. Each time a flap is opened, encourage the children to tell you what they can see and to make a guess as to what they think the picture is of. Stimulate discussion by giving the children a few clues such as, 'The picture is of an animal that is found in many homes'. If the children have not already guessed what the picture is by the time the last flap is opened, give each child a last chance to say what they think it is before removing the covering card to reveal the picture underneath.

Finish by talking about the picture and what the children think of it.

Support
Keep the number of flaps to a minimum of three and ensure that the pictures chosen will be easily recognizable by the children.

Extension
Encourage older children to make their own peek-a-boo pictures for the rest of the group.

GROUP SIZE
Four children.

TIMING
15 to 20 minutes.

MY DIARY

Learning objectives
To enjoy listening to and using spoken and written language; to know that print carries meaning and, in English, is read from left to right and top to bottom.

What you need
A4 sheets of paper, A4 sheets of coloured card; coloured pencils; pen; lengths of ribbon; glue; spreaders; current photograph of each child; scissors; marker pen; hole-punch.

Preparation
Make a 'diary' for each child by placing one sheet of coloured card flat on a table and placing a number of A4 sheets of white paper on top of it, ensuring that each book has the same amount of pages. Fold all the sheets of paper in half before punching two holes in the middle of the folded side of the book. Thread a piece of ribbon through these holes, tie a knot and finish off with a bow. Number each of the pages in order and write each child's name and the year on the front cover. Finish by asking each child to stick a photo of themselves under their name.

What to do
Set aside a time during the course of every week when you sit quietly with a group of children at a table to hear their news. Ask the children to describe in detail what they did the day before and stress that it is important for everyone to listen to each other when someone else is speaking. When the children have finished talking, hand out their diaries and place the coloured pencils in the centre of the table. Ask the children to turn to a clean page and to draw the news that they have just told you about on that page. Once each child's picture is complete, encourage further discussion by asking the child to tell you about their picture. Write down exactly what they tell you making sure that you record the date in the top right-hand corner of the page. When you have finished writing, read what you have written back to them running your fingers under each word as you read, emphasizing a left to right sequence. The children will also realize that the events are recorded on pages that are numbered.

When the books are finished, ask each child to tell you what they did on, say, page 4 of their diary.

Support
Limit the above activity to just once a week for the younger children.

Extension
Older children should be encouraged to number the pages of their diary themselves and to read a page of their book to another child in the group.

HOME LINKS

Ask parents and carers to draw their children's attention to the sequential order of page numbers when reading a story, as well as running their fingers under the text as they read.

RUGBY SHIRT LINE UP

Learning objective
To use talk to organize and sequence ideas.

What you need
A4 sheets of coloured card; the photocopiable sheet on page 67; string; scissors; marker pen; four dowelling rods; sticky-backed plastic.

Preparation
Copy the photocopiable sheet onto pieces of card by feeding them through a photocopier, making sure that you have sixteen rugby shirts. Number the first eight shirts 1 to 8, and the second eight shirts 1 to 8, making sure that both sets are identical to each other. In addition to the number, write the corresponding number word on each shirt. Cover the shirts with sticky-backed plastic before cutting them out. To make a clothes line, knot a piece of string to the top of one dowelling rod and stretch across the table, making sure that the string is long enough to hold eight shirts, before attaching the other end to a second dowelling rod. Make a second clothes line in the same manner.

What to do
Place the first clothes line across the top of the table, and peg up one set of shirts. Place the second line under the first one and ask one of the children to peg up an identical row to the one displayed, using the second set of shirts. Encourage a left to right sequence. Talk to the children as they work saying, for example, 'Which number shirt comes 'first', 'second,' 'before,' 'after'?' and so on. When the shirts have been placed in the correct order, ask the children various questions such as, 'What colour is the shirt with a number 1 on it?' and 'What number shirt comes before the white one?'. Once the children know what is expected of them, ask one child to 'hang' the shirts on the first clothes line in whatever order they choose and then ask another child to repeat the order. The other children can watch to see if the second child makes any mistakes.

Support
Limit the number of shirts to groups of just four and slowly increase this number.

Extension
Mix up the shirts and ask the children to place them in their correct numerical order. A further extension would be to let one child study the shirts on the line, remove them and then replace them in exactly the same order as before.

GROUP SIZE
Small groups.

TIMING
15 to 20 minutes.

HOME LINKS
Encourage the children to learn to clap the name of their siblings and other family members and to show their skills at home.

MULTICULTURAL LINKS
Invite parents and carers of different nationalities to visit your setting and ask them to say a few words in their native tongue, thereby drawing children's attention to speech patterns of different cultures.

SPEECH PATTERNS

Learning objectives

To explore and experiment with sounds and words; to sustain attentive listening and respond to what they have heard by relevant actions.

What you need

The photocopiable sheet on page 68.

Preparation

For the purpose of this activity, the children will need to be familiar with body percussion as well as rhythmic speech pattern exercises. The best way of introducing this is to start by saying each child's name and accompanying it with clapping. For example, Anne = one clap, Rak-esh = two claps and so on. Say each child's name separately, accompanied by clapping, and ask the child to clap their name back to you. The children will have great fun with this and it is a good way of taking the daily register, as the children tend to listen carefully for their name to be called out. Extend this further by clapping and saying a short rhythmic phrase and asking the children to answer, for example:

Adult: 'Pe–ter, Pe–ter,   where are you?'

Child: 'Here I am,   here I am.'

Once the children have mastered the above they will be ready to move on to the activity.

What to do

Sit with a small group of children on the floor and teach them the words of the speech pattern on the photocopiable sheet on page 68. Encourage them to listen carefully to what is being said. Once they are familiar with the speech pattern, introduce the accompanying body percussion, at first using just clapping for both lines. Once the children have mastered this, introduce a knee-slapping accompaniment for the second line. Ask the children if they can think of other parts of their bodies that they could use to accompany the speech pattern. Experiment by changing the body percussion accompaniment to whatever is suitable for your group.

Support

This activity is best done in groups of no more than three children.

Extension

Ask older children to think of simple questions that they can ask each other accompanied by body percussion.

GROUP SIZE
Three children.

TIMING
20 minutes.

CRACK THE SAFE

Learning objectives
To listen and use spoken language in their learning; to respond to what they have heard by relevant actions.

What you need
Shoebox; silver paint; paintbrush; eight ping-pong balls; marker pen; play money; selection of plastic jewellery; scissors; shallow basket; eight small sticky labels.

Preparation
Make a 'safe' by painting a shoebox and lid with silver paint. While the paint is drying, write the number symbols 1 to 8 on each of the eight ping-pong balls before placing in a shallow basket. Once the paint on the safe is dry, cut out eight circular holes, in two rows of four each in the top of the box making sure that the holes are big enough to allow the balls to fit through. Write the number symbols 1 to 8 on the small labels and place one above each of the holes in the lid in their correct order. Cut another hole in one side of the box, which must be big enough for a child's hand to fit through. Place a selection of plastic jewellery and paper money inside the box before placing the lid on top of the safe.

What to do
Place the safe and basket of balls on the table and tell the children that there are many surprises locked inside the safe. In order to find out what is inside the safe we need to be able to remember a number combination, that will change each time the safe is 'cracked'.

Ask one of the children to listen carefully to what you say, and to repeat exactly a simple three-digit combination. If they repeat the combination correctly then they must find the corresponding balls in the basket and put them into the correct number holes in the top of the safe. They have now cracked the safe and can put their hand into the hole in the side of the box and remove one of the objects inside – either a piece of jewellery or money. Take the lid off the safe, remove the ping-pong balls and continue. If the child cannot remember the combination in sequence, try again using fewer numbers.

Support
Keep the number combinations very simple.

Extension
Older children will enjoy playing with a partner by taking turns to ask each other simple combinations.

HOME LINKS
Suggest to parents and carers that while they are out with their children, they call out two- or three-digit number combinations from car number plates and ask their children to repeat them.

GROUP SIZE
Small groups.

TIMING
15 to 20 minutes.

LET'S SING!

Learning objective
To listen with enjoyment and respond to songs.

What you need
Pieces of coloured card; felt-tipped pens; tape recorder; tape; coloured pencils; scissors; copy of the song 'Five Little Froggies' from *This Little Puffin…* compiled by Elizabeth Matterson (Puffin Books); the photocopiable sheet on page 69; display board.

Preparation
Make a copy of the photocopiable sheet on page 69 and enlarge it as required. Ask the children to colour the pictures using the coloured pencils before cutting along the bold lines to make flashcards.

What to do
Teach the children the song 'Five Little Froggies' and once they are familiar with it, show them the flashcards that show the sequence of verses in the song. Ask the children to place the cards in their correct order on the display board. Sing the song with the children and encourage them to accompany their singing with clapping or other body percussion. Record the children's singing using the tape recorder and play it back to the children so that they can listen to it themselves. Once the children know the song, encourage them to act it out. They will enjoy being 'added' or 'subtracted' according to the verse and counting with their whole body.

Support
Younger children will need to have the song repeated a number of times in order to become familiar with it. The important thing is the pleasure that they gain from listening to the rhyme and the rhythm of the language.

Extension
Encourage the children to make up their own number songs, which if possible, you should write down exactly as heard.

HOME LINKS
Ask parents and carers to find other frog songs, such as 'Five Little Speckled Frogs' that they can sing with their children.

GROUP SIZE
Four children.

GROUP SIZE
Four children.

TIMING
20 minutes.

WHY DOES IT FLOAT?

Learning objectives
To use talk to organize, sequence and clarify thinking; to interact with others negotiating activities.

What you need
A3 sheet of card; marker pen; large clear plastic bowl; plastic bottles of different sizes with screw-on lids; the photocopiable sheet on page 70; marker pen; aprons; water; plastic jug; sticky-backed plastic; plastic table-cloth.

Preparation
Copy and enlarge the 'Float and sink experiment' on the photocopiable sheet on page 70 to A3 size before covering with sticky-backed plastic.

Cover a table with a plastic table-cloth and place a plastic jug filled with water, a bowl and a collection of plastic bottles on the table. Write a number on the outside of each bottle and the corresponding number on its lid using the permanent marker pen.

What to do
Ensure that each child is wearing an apron. Place the chart where all the children can see it and explain that the steps of the experiment are numbered and that you start at the top of the page at 'Step 1'. Place your finger under 'Step 1' and read out loud what it says, running your finger underneath the words to draw the children's attention to them.

Take the plastic jug and pour the water into the bowl. Read 'Step 2' out loud and ask the children to predict what they think will happen when you place the bottle in the water without a lid on it.

Encourage the children to talk freely and ask questions that will stimulate discussion such as, 'Why do you think the bottle sank?'. The children will come up with various reasons, some of them being closer to the actual explanation than others. Explain that water has filled the bottle and the weight from the water has made the bottle sink. Proceed to 'Step 3' and finally to 'Step 4.' During the course of the experiment, explain that when the lid is replaced on the bottle it floats as air has filled the bottle and this makes it float. Draw the children's attention to the numbers on the bottles and the corresponding lids and make them aware that the lids will only fit onto the bottles with the same number.

Support
Limit the number of children taking part to no more than two.

Extension
Repeat by asking the children to tell you the steps of the experiment in the correct sequence by looking at the chart.

HOME LINKS
Let the children take home copies of the experiment on the photocopiable sheet so that parents and carers can try it with them.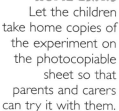

Mathematical development

The ideas in this chapter encourage children to use developing mathematical ideas and vocabulary to work through fun practical problems. There is a fishing game with numbered fishes and an estimation activity guessing sweets in a jar, as well as many other original ideas.

GROUP SIZE
Small groups.

TIMING
15 minutes.

HOME LINKS
Ask parents and carers to let their children count pieces of vegetables or other food items served at mealtimes. For example, 'Three sprouts for Mum and six sprouts for Dad'.

PLATES OF NUMBERS

Learning objectives
To order numbers from 0 to 10; to count reliably up to ten everyday objects.

What you need
Eleven paper plates; marker pen; selection of buttons in different sizes; shallow cardboard box; coloured sticky dots; ten pieces of card (approximately 7cm x 13cm); sticky-backed plastic; the photocopiable sheet on page 71.

Preparation
Stick coloured dots on ten of the paper plates – none on the first plate and one dot on the second plate, through to ten dots on the eleventh plate. Place a selection of buttons in different sizes in a shallow cardboard box. Number the pieces of card with numerals 1 to 10 and cover with sticky-backed plastic.

What to do
Shuffle the plates and place in a pile on a table along with the container of buttons and the number cards. Ask each child in turn to pick up a plate and to count the number of dots on it. Explain that the numeral tells us how many buttons we need. Ask them to count out that amount of buttons and place them on the plate. Continue until all the plates are full, except one, and all the children have had a turn. Encourage the children to place these plates in their correct numerical order and match them to the number cards. Ask the children to take turns showing you the plate with the same amount of buttons on as their age. Return the buttons to the container and repeat, so that each child has a turn with a different number. Give each child a copy of the photocopiable sheet on page 71 to complete.

Support
Limit the plates to between one and five.

Extension
Give each child a plate with a different number written on it and ask them to put the corresponding amount of buttons on it. Ask the children to place the plates in their correct numerical order and to find the correct number card to go underneath it.

FISHING GAME

Learning objectives

To recognize amounts and numerals 1 to 10; to sort in correct numerical order.

What you need

Piece of dowelling rod; string; magnet; envelope; ten paper clips, shoebox; blue paint; paintbrush; scissors; coloured construction card; the photocopiable sheet on page 72; coloured sticky dots; hole-punch; marker pen; number cards from the 'Plates of numbers' activity on page 25.

Preparation

Make a 'fishing rod' by tying a magnet to one end of a piece of string and attaching the other end to a dowelling rod. Copy the photocopiable sheet on page 72 onto the coloured card and cut out the fish, punching a hole near each fish's mouth and hooking with a paper clip. Store the fishing rod and fish in an envelope and paint a shoebox blue.

What to do

Place the shoebox containing the fish in the centre of the room with the number cards in their correct numerical order alongside the box as a number line. Show the children how to 'fish' for numbers, explaining that if more than one fish is caught at any one time, the second fish must be thrown back into the 'water'. Give one of the four children the fishing rod and invite them to take a turn to catch a fish. When a fish has been caught, ask the child to take it off the fishing rod and to count the number of dots on it. Take the fish over to the number line and place it underneath the correct number. The second child takes a turn and so the game continues until all the fish in the box have been 'caught' and are in their correct position on the number line. To make the game more interesting, make a boat shape from a large piece of cardboard and tape it to the floor with the fish spread around the boat on the floor. Each of the children has a turn to sit on the boat and fish 'over the side'.

Support

Limit the number of fish to be caught at first, then increase the number gradually.

Extension

Place the fish in a hula hoop on the floor so that the dots are clearly visible. Ask each child to take a turn to catch a fish with the number of dots on it as called out by either you or another child in the group.

GROUP SIZE
Ten children.

TIMING
15 minutes.

BAGS OF NUMBERS

Learning objectives

To use language such as 'more' or 'less' to compare two sets of objects; to recognize which numbers come 'before' and 'after' a number from 1 to 10.

What you need

A collection of coloured buttons; A4 clear plastic zip wallets; 1 to 10 number cards from the 'Plates of numbers' activity on page 25; a shallow container for the buttons.

Preparation

Place different amounts of buttons in zip wallets, ranging from just one button per bag to ten. Zip each bag closed and draw a vertical line down the centre of the bag from the zip end to the bottom using a permanent marker pen.

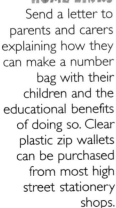

What to do

Place the number cards in a pile in the middle of a table along with the zip wallets or 'number bags'. Explain to the children that each bag has a different amount of buttons inside. Show them how to move the buttons from one side of the bag to the other to create different set combinations. Invite each child to pick up a bag, count the total amount of buttons inside and to tell everyone how many buttons there are. Encourage the children to experiment by moving the buttons around and observing that you can have, for example, five buttons on one side of the vertical line and none on the other side, or two buttons on one side of the vertical line and three on the other side, yet in both instances you still have just five buttons in the bag. Once the children are confident, ask them to find the correct numeral card from the pile on the table that represents the total number of buttons in their bag, and to place it underneath the bag on the table. Continue by placing all the bags in their correct numerical order. When this has been completed, ask questions such as, 'What number comes before five? ...after six?' and so on.

Support

Start with just three bags and slowly increase the number as the children's skills improve.

Extension

Invite the children to tell you how many ways their buttons can be shared out. A child with five buttons could tell you, 'Five and none, four and one, three and two...' and so on.

HOME LINKS
Send a letter to parents and carers explaining how they can make a number bag with their children and the educational benefits of doing so. Clear plastic zip wallets can be purchased from most high street stationery shops.

NUMBER TINS

Learning objectives
To begin to compare number quantities; to recognize numerals and identify amounts of 0 to 10; to order numbers from 0 to 10.

What you need
Eleven small tins, approximately 10cm in height; plain contact paper in one colour; coloured dot stickers; marker pen; straws in different colours; a large shallow container.

Preparation
Clean the tins before use and then cover with contact paper of the same colour to avoid confusing the children. Number one side of each tin with numerals from 0 to 10 and on the reverse stick on the corresponding number of coloured dots. Place the straws in a shallow container.

What to do
Place the tins on a table in random order with the numbers facing the children, placing the container of straws close by. Ask the first child to tell you the number on the tin directly in front of them. Explain that they can turn the tin round and count the dots on the reverse side if they are not sure. The first child takes a turn to place the same number of straws into the tin as the numeral indicates. Repeat, with the next child taking a turn with the second tin in the line. While they work, the children can check each other, and themselves, to see if they are correct by counting the number of dots on the reverse of each tin. Continue until all the tins have straws in them except the one with '0' on it, which will remain empty. This is an excellent way of introducing children to the concept of '0'.

Invite the children to place the tins in their correct numerical order following a left to right sequence. Once this is complete, ask questions such as 'Which tin has the least amount of straws inside and which has the most?'; 'If I remove the tin with the most straws inside (number 10) which tin will now have the most straws inside?' and so on.

Support
Let the children experiment with only four tins and straws and slowly increase the number as they become more proficient.

Extension
Place the tins numbered 2 and 6 on the table and ask the children to take turns placing the remaining tins in their correct numerical order. This activity can be done by putting any number of tins on the table, even just one, and asking the children to fill in the spaces with the other tins in their correct order.

CATHY THE CATERPILLAR

Learning objective
To arrange numbers sequentially.

What you need
Permanent marker pen; sticky-backed plastic; A3 length of cardboard; circular disc; two small white wooden blocks; scissors; coloured dot stickers; an envelope.

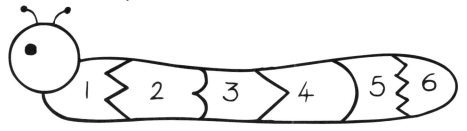

Preparation
Take an A3 length of cardboard and draw a long wide caterpillar shape onto it. Divide the 'caterpillar' into six sections by drawing vertical wavy lines evenly spaced along the caterpillar. Starting with number 1, label each section of the caterpillar in order, finishing with number 6. On the reverse side of each numbered section of the caterpillar, stick on the equivalent amount of coloured dots. Carefully cut along the lines that you have drawn, making sure that the sections can be easily reassembled. Attach a circular 'head' to section 1 of the caterpillar and draw a face on both sides. Place the caterpillar into an envelope. Make a dice by writing the numbers 1 to 6 on one of the white wooden blocks, and on the other block draw one to six dots.

What to do
Lay the caterpillar pieces on the table starting with the dot side facing upwards. The first child in the group throws the dice with the dots on it and counts out loud how many dots are visible. If they do not get a '1', the next child takes a turn and so on, until a '1' is thrown. This child must then identify the puzzle piece with one dot on it to start the puzzle. Continue in this manner until all six pieces have been placed in their correct order. Encourage the children who are not having a turn to check that the correct pieces of puzzle are being picked up.

Turn the puzzle over and complete it again, this time using the number dice and correct puzzle number piece. This is a self-correcting activity, as the pieces will fit together in only one way.

Support
Use just the dot side of the puzzle and corresponding dice until the children become used to what is expected of them.

Extension
Play the caterpillar game with the numbered puzzle pieces and the dice with dots on. Repeat by turning the caterpillar over and matching the dots on the puzzle pieces to the dice with numbers on it. Encourage the child to play the game on their own.

HOME LINKS
Ask parents and carers to play a traditional number game, such as Snakes and Ladders with their children.

MULTICULTURAL LINKS
Play the game using a Chinese New Year's dragon shape in place of a caterpillar.

GROUP SIZE
Four children.

TIMING
15 to 20 minutes.

GUESS HOW MANY

Learning objectives
To begin to make estimations to solve practical problems; to begin to use mathematical vocabulary in practical activities and discussion.

What you need
Five clear plastic jars; a collection of different items such as five pencil sharpeners, two buttons and so on; five large sheets of paper; coloured pencils; the photocopiable sheet on page 73; marker pen.

Preparation
Place different quantities of small items ranging from one to five in separate clear plastic jars. Divide each of the five sheets of paper into squares – five vertically and four horizontally – in which to record the children's estimations. Write each child's name along the bottom of the graph and numbers 1 to 5 up the side.

What to do
Place the jars in any order on a table and tell them that they will be making careful guesses about amounts of objects. Explain that there will never be more than five items in any jar, otherwise their estimations will be way outside the range.

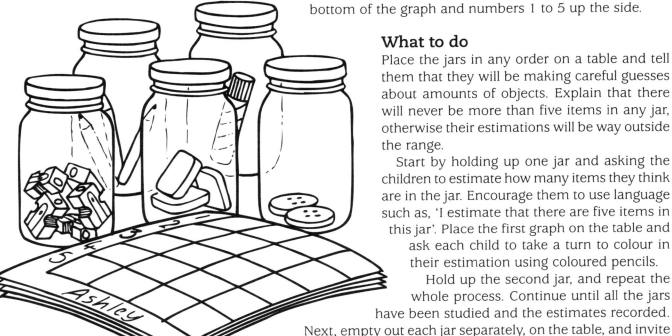

Start by holding up one jar and asking the children to estimate how many items they think are in the jar. Encourage them to use language such as, 'I estimate that there are five items in this jar'. Place the first graph on the table and ask each child to take a turn to colour in their estimation using coloured pencils.

Hold up the second jar, and repeat the whole process. Continue until all the jars have been studied and the estimates recorded. Next, empty out each jar separately, on the table, and invite the children to count each group of items. Show the children each corresponding graph that they have filled out and see who, if anyone, was correct. If no one estimated the correct amount, ask the children to identify whose estimation was the closest. Encourage the children to use vocabulary such as 'estimate', 'graph' and so on. Finish by giving each child a copy of the photocopiable sheet on page 73 for them to complete.

Support
Concentrate on estimating the contents of just two jars. Slowly increase the number of jars, as the estimations become more accurate.

Extension
Have more than one jar with the same amount of items inside, the sizes of which are different. The children will be amazed that both jars contain the same quantity. Explain that even though items come in different sizes, for example, 'six cars' and 'six buttons, 'six' remains 'six', regardless of the size of the items involved.

HOME LINKS
Ask parents and carers to encourage estimation skills at home, such as asking their children to estimate how many spoons they think are in the cutlery draw. Count them together to see if they are correct.

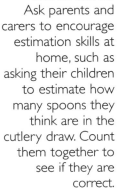

MULTICULTURAL LINKS
Make a large group puzzle using Arabic numerals (see the photocopiable sheet on page 74 for reference).

NUMBER PUZZLES

Learning objective
To recognize numerals, words and amounts 1 to 10.

What you need
Ten pieces of thick card, approximately 17cm x 20cm; marker pen; sticky coloured shapes; sticky-backed plastic.

Preparation
Divide each of the ten cards in half by drawing different lines across each one, making sure that the joining edge of each pair of cards is unique so that they cannot be matched incorrectly. On one half of each of the pieces of card, write a numeral between 1 and 10 as well as the number word. On the other half, stick on the corresponding amount of sticky coloured shapes, such as two dots, three small bell shapes and so on. Cover with sticky-backed plastic and cut each card into pieces following the lines drawn on the card.

What to do
Mix up the card pieces and place them in random order facing upward on a table. Invite two children to take turns to pick up a card and count out loud the number of shapes on it, and then to find the matching half with the correct numeral and written word on it. The puzzles are self-correcting in that they will fit together in only one way and the children will know if they have chosen the correct puzzle piece or not. Once the puzzles have been completed, place them in their correct numerical order, drawing the children's attention to the written word and number on each one. Reinforce vocabulary by using words such as, 'This puzzle comes first in the line and this one comes second...' and so on.

Support
Give the children just five puzzles to fit together.

Extension
Ask the children to make their own number puzzles using small pictures cut from toy catalogues. Encourage them to let another child complete the puzzle that they have made.

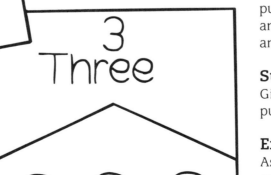

TOY NUMBER LINE UP

Learning objective

To understand the relation between numerals and actual amounts of things.

What you need

Ten shoeboxes; a variety of small toys; marker pen.

Preparation

Label two sets of shoeboxes in sequence starting with number 1 and finishing with number 5. Place collections of small toys in easy-to-find places around the room.

What to do

Give each of the ten children one of the boxes numbered 1 to 5. Ask them to look carefully at the number on their box and then to walk around the room choosing toys, the number of which corresponds to the number on their box. For example, if their box has a 4 on it, they must collect four toy cars. Once they have finished collecting their toys, gather the children around a table and ask if they can find the other child in the group who has the same number printed on their box as them. Starting with number 1, ask both children to lay their collection of toys out on the table. Check that the correct amounts of toys have been collected by laying both sets alongside each other in one-to-one correspondence.

Support

Divide the children into pairs and ask them to collect the required amount of items with a partner. They will then be able to check the number of items required by counting them out and working with another child.

Extension

Encourage the children to collect specific items, thereby improving their memory skills.

CHAPTER 4

This chapter provides a range of activities which highlight the importance of numbers in our everyday environment. Ideas include making a simple calendar and observing the progression of days, creating a role-play supermarket and delivering letters to numbered post-boxes.

Knowledge and understanding of the world

GROUP SIZE
Whole group.

TIMING
20 to 25 minutes.

HOME LINKS
Ask parents and carers to show their children a calendar at home and how appointments, special occasions, holidays and so on are recorded on it.

MULTICULTURAL LINKS
Record multicultural festivals on your calendar.

LET'S MAKE A CALENDAR

Learning objective
To observe the sequence of days and dates on a calendar.

What you need
Display board; two sheets of A3 coloured card; coloured pencils; marker pen; ruler; Blu-Tack.

Preparation
Select a month and divide a sheet of A3 card into the correct amount of days by drawing squares on it. Number each square with the correct date by copying a calendar. Find out if any of the children have birthdays or if there are any special occasions that month and record these underneath the appropriate dates. Cut the second sheet of card into the equivalent amount of squares to cover the spaces on the calendar.

What to do
Attach the calendar to a display board at child height and place the coloured pencils and cards on a table. Explain to the children that we know what date it is by looking at our calendar. Tell them how the months of the year are a continuous cycle and that this is why our birthdays and Christmas come around once a year on a set date. Give each child a square of coloured card and ask them to draw a picture using the coloured pencils. Attach a small piece of Blu-Tack to each picture and stick one over each number on the calendar. Make a special time every day when the children are given a turn to remove a picture card, in correct sequence, to reveal the number underneath. Every time a number below eleven is revealed, ask them to tell you what it is. See if the children can tell you which number will follow the one revealed and which number came before. Most of the children will just enjoy seeing the numbers as they are revealed and seeing how each day of the week appears underneath the one before it. Draw the children's attention to the special occasions recorded on the calendar.

Support
In order to avoid confusing the younger children, start by making a 'Days of the week' chart.

Extension
Older children could make a calendar for every month of the year.

GROUP SIZE
Small groups.

TIMING
20 to 25 minutes.

SHOPPING SPREE

Learning objective
To investigate uses of numbers in everyday life.

What you need
Empty food boxes and packets; plastic bottles in a variety of sizes; string; plastic fruit and vegetables; paper plates; strips of card; scissors; paper bags; small baskets; food trays; a toy cash register; overall; sticky tape; play money of different denominations; purse; coloured marker pens; small stick-on labels; three tables; small squares of card; the photocopiable sheet on page 58.

Preparation
Discuss with the children beforehand what sort of shop they would like to set up in the role-play area and plan accordingly. For the purpose of this activity, the shop will be a supermarket. Send out a letter to parents and carers asking them to collect clean empty food boxes, packets and plastic bottles in different sizes. Make a selection of signs for the supermarket such as, 'Special offer – was 10p, now 5p', and a large sign showing the supermarket name. Write price labels on small pieces of folded card, like place settings, and stick-on labels. Keep amounts simple and low. Lay out three tables in an 'L' shape, suspending the shop sign with string above the tables. The other signs should be attached to the front of the tables with sticky tape so that they are clearly visible. Place the shopping baskets on the floor next to the first table and the paper bags on the last table along with the toy cash register and shop assistant's overall. Place some play money in the purse and the rest in the cash register.

What to do
Start by reading the poem 'At the supermarket' on the photocopiable sheet on page 58 to the children to introduce the topic with plenty of relevant vocabulary. Encourage the children to help sort the food into groups and display this on the tables in the food trays and paper plates with the stick-on and folded price labels. Let the children take turns to be the shop assistant, shopper, shelf-stacker, packer and so on.

While the children are busy doing their shopping, ask them which item is the most expensive in the shop, the cheapest and so on. Ask them to buy items of a specific price in order to see if they are able to recognize different numbers.

Support
Encourage younger children to practice number skills by buying just one item at a time and counting out the exact amount of 'money' when they pay. Play 'in role' yourself to help the action along.

Extension
Ask older children to add the total cost of their purchases together and to see if they will get any change.

HOME LINKS
Ask parents and carers to draw their children's attention to how items are individually priced in different shops so that we know how much they are going to cost. Suggest that their children help them to make a shopping list the next time they do their weekly shop.

MULTICULTURAL LINKS
Set up a shop selling multicultural clothing or an Indian or Chinese restaurant.

GROUP SIZE
Small groups.

TIMING
25 to 30 minutes.

HOME LINKS
Ask parents to allow their child to help with the baking of a simple recipe at home and to point out the changes that take place during cooking.

STAINED GLASS NUMBER BISCUITS

Learning objectives

To find out about, and identify some features of events that they observe; to ask questions about why things happen and how things work.

What you need

Boiled sweets; 100g (4oz) butter or margarine; 75g (3oz) wholewheat flour; 75g (3oz) plain flour; 40g (1 ½ oz) icing sugar; baking tray; number cutters; blunt knife; mixing bowl; rolling pin; baking board; wire rack; greaseproof paper; rice paper; sieve; pen; aprons.

Preparation

Ensure that you have all the ingredients and utensils required for the activity beforehand and that everything is laid out in an inviting manner. Preheat the oven to 180°C (350°F or Gas Mark 4) and place a sheet of greaseproof paper on a baking tray. Cut the rice paper into squares and write the children's names on them, one per child.

What to do

Ensure that all of the children have washed their hands and are wearing aprons. Ask the children to take turns helping you so that they all try at least one stage of the process. Cream the butter and sugar together in a large bowl, making sure that you get rid of most of the lumps. Sift the flour into the mixture and knead gently until you make a firm dough, adding a small amount of water if it is too stiff. Remove the dough from the bowl and place on a lightly-floured board before rolling it out, making sure that it is not too thin. Using the knife, cut the dough into a number of rectangular shapes.

The pieces must be big enough for the number cutters to be used on the inside of each one leaving a border around the edge. Invite each child to choose one of the number cutters and to press down firmly in the centre of one of the rectangle shapes. Place each shape on a baking tray along with each child's name. Bake on the middle shelf of the oven for approximately five minutes. Remove from the oven in order to place one boiled sweet in the middle of each biscuit. Take care, as the tray will be hot. Return to the oven for a further five minutes. Once the biscuits are cooked, take the tray out of the oven and place the biscuits on the baking rack to cool.

During the making of the biscuits talk to the children about the changes that the mixture undertakes before, during and after the cooking process. They will be amazed at how the sweets melt in the heat of the oven and then harden again once they cool down. The children can also talk about the numbers that they have made.

Support

Work with no more than two or three children.

Extension

Encourage older children to follow a simple pictorial recipe.

GROUP SIZE
Whole group.

TIMING
20 to 25 minutes.

ABACUS

Learning objectives
To build and construct with a range of objects; to select tools and techniques to shape and assemble the materials that they are using.

What you need
The photocopiable sheet on page 79; play dough ingredients; thick skewers; greased baking tray; wire rack; five dowelling rods of the same length; airtight containers; old boot box; scissors; paint; paintbrushes; envelope; ten corks; small pieces of card; marker pen.

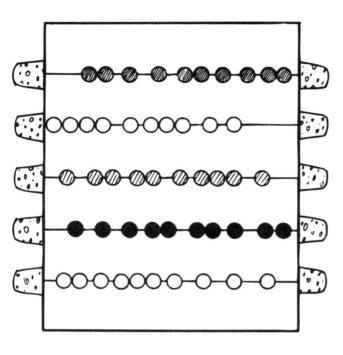

Preparation
Make five batches of fresh play dough in different colours (by adding food colouring), using the play dough recipe on the photocopiable sheet on page 79, and place in airtight containers until required. Number a set of cards from 1 to 10 (or use the number cards from the 'Plates of numbers' activity on page 25 in Chapter 3) and place in an envelope. Paint the boot box in a bright colour. Once dry, make five holes using scissors, equally spaced in the long sides of the box starting about 5cm from the top. Make holes in one end of each of the ten corks using a pair of scissors.

What to do
Invite the children to make beads for the abacus using coloured play dough. It is not necessary to separate the children's beads from each other as all of the beads are going to be used collectively to make a group abacus. Make sure that the skewers used are thicker than the dowelling rods or the beads will not go on. Push the first dowelling rod into the top hole on the left-hand side of the box and cover the end with a cork. While holding the rod, encourage the children to help feed ten beads, of the same colour, onto the rod making sure that the beads move easily. Once the beads are threaded, push the other end of the rod through the corresponding hole in the other side of the box and place a second cork over that end to hold it in place. Continue in this manner until all five rods have been threaded with ten coloured beads.

Divide the children into smaller groups so that they can experiment with the abacus. Show them how they can move the beads around and ask them to count out loud the number of beads on each rod.

Support
Younger children will have great fun counting the beads and moving them from side to side.

HOME LINKS
Ask parents and carers to show their children how people work out problems on a calculator.

Extension
Place the envelope containing the number cards on the table and ask one child to take a card from inside. Move the beads to the right-hand side of the box before asking the child what number card they are holding. Invite them to move the correct amount of beads from the right-hand side to the left-hand side of the box, and ask them to tell you how many beads now remain on the right.

THE SAME AND DIFFERENT

Learning objectives

To look closely at similarities and differences between themselves and others; to observe and identify specific features of other people.

What you need

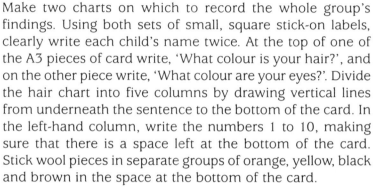

Display board; two A3 sheets of card; marker pen; orange, black, brown and yellow wool; scissors; two sets of small, square stick-on labels; glue; spreader; coloured felt-tipped pens; small non-breakable hand mirrors.

Preparation

Make two charts on which to record the whole group's findings. Using both sets of small, square stick-on labels, clearly write each child's name twice. At the top of one of the A3 pieces of card write, 'What colour is your hair?', and on the other piece write, 'What colour are your eyes?'. Divide the hair chart into five columns by drawing vertical lines from underneath the sentence to the bottom of the card. In the left-hand column, write the numbers 1 to 10, making sure that there is a space left at the bottom of the card. Stick wool pieces in separate groups of orange, yellow, black and brown in the space at the bottom of the card.

Make an eye colour chart by dividing the second sheet of card into four columns and writing the numbers 1 to 10 down the left-hand side of the card. Draw a blue, brown and green eye along the bottom of the remaining three columns.

What colour are your eyes?			
10			
9			
8			
7			
6			
5			
4			
3			Bruce
2		Diana	Maddy
1		Alexia	Bronwyn
			👁

What to do

Place the hand mirrors on a low table and ask each child to have a turn at looking at themselves in the mirror. Encourage observation skills by asking them if we all look the same and how we are similar and different from each other. Encourage the children to describe each other in a positive manner and stress that we are actually more alike than different from each other. Introduce classification by asking all the children who have blonde hair to stand together in a group, all those with black hair in another group and so on until you have covered each hair colour.

Attach the 'Hair colour chart' at the children's level on a display board and ask each child in turn which colour wool they think is the closest to their own hair colour. Help them to identify the closest match. Give each child a label with their name on it and ask them to stick this label in the column that they think is the same colour as their hair. Complete the 'Eye colour chart' in the same manner. Ask the children to count how many children in the group have the same colour hair and eyes as them.

Support

Let younger children complete just one or the other chart.

Extension

Encourage older children to count the different groups and tell you which categories have the most, least and same amount of people in them. They can then write this information on label to attach to the side of each chart.

HOME LINKS

Ask parents and carers to make a similar chart at home where their children can record the similarities and differences between themselves and other family members. Remain sensitive to individual family situations.

MULTICULTURAL LINKS

Make a 'People of the world' chart to record the difference in either the hair, skin or eye colour between people of different countries by looking through library books.

WEIGH IT UP

Learning objective

To find out about and make comparisons between features of objects that they observe.

What you need

Display board; non-fungicide wallpaper roll; felt-tipped pens; stick-on suction hook; masking tape; thick sewing elastic; small plastic bucket with handle; sticky dots; plastic baskets; marker pen; ten identical small toy cars and wooden blocks.

Preparation

Measure one piece of wallpaper roll against the display board at child height and cut off the required length. Turn the piece of wallpaper over so that the plain side is facing upwards before dividing the piece of paper in half. At the top of the paper, draw a picture of a toy car on the left-hand side and a picture of a small wooden block on the right-hand side. Attach this paper to the display board using pieces of masking tape on all four corners. A few feet above the centre line on the paper, attach the stick-on suction hook making sure that it is secure by placing two strips of masking tape across the top and bottom. Tie one end of a piece of elastic to the handle of a small bucket and attach the other end to the hook. Place the toy cars in one basket and the wooden blocks in the other.

What to do

Explain to the children that different things weigh different amounts and that one object weighs less than two of the same object, and three weighs more than two and so on. Start with the toy cars, showing the children how to place one car in the bucket and to draw a line where the bottom of the bucket hangs. Write '1' next to the line and place one coloured dot next to it. Continue by adding another car to the bucket and seeing where the bucket now sits. Remove one of the cars in order to show that the bucket will move back up to the same position it was in before the second car was placed inside. Ask, 'Is it lower or higher than before?', 'Why is there a difference?'.

Continue recording your findings until all ten cars have been weighed and marked on the chart. While the children are weighing the cars, talk about how the more you have of something the heavier it is, and the less you have the lighter it is.

Repeat using the second chart with the wooden blocks. Point out the difference between the lines made for the weight of the cars and the wooden blocks.

Support

Use only one chart for younger children and limit the amount of cars or blocks to just six.

Extension

Encourage older children to use mathematical vocabulary such as, 'I'm adding another car to the bucket' or 'If I take away two cars from the bucket where will it hang now?'. Allow them to experiment on their own by making additional charts and weighing different items.

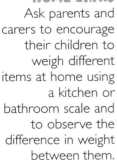

GROUP SIZE
Six children.

GROUP SIZE
Six children.

TIMING
15 to 20 minutes.

FEELY NUMBER BOX

Learning objective

To investigate objects and materials using all of their senses as appropriate.

What you need

Twelve pieces of thick card, sandpaper; scissors; one shoebox with lid; six shoeboxes without lids; stick-on labels; paint; paintbrushes; glue; spreader; marker pen.

Preparation

Cut two sets of 1 to 6 number symbols from sandpaper and attach one to each of the twelve pieces of card. Clearly label each of the six shoeboxes with a number from 1 to 6. Make a feely box by painting a shoebox and lid in a bright colour. When the paint is dry, cut a hole in one side of the box ensuring that a child's hand can fit inside. Stick one set of the number cards to the shoebox lid and place the other set inside the box.

What to do

Place the numbered boxes in random order on the floor around a low table with the number box on it. Explain to the children how blind people are able to read by feeling raised print that is called Braille. Ask each child to place one hand inside the shoebox and to feel one of the cards without looking. With the other hand, ask the child to feel the number cards on top of the box to see if they can identify the card that matches the one inside the box by touch alone. Allow the children time to practise the activity.

When they think that they have identified the correct card, remove it from the box to see if they are correct. If they are, remove the card and ask the child to place it in the correct shoebox next to the table. Allow the other children to have a turn until all the cards have been correctly identified. Once complete, ask each child to pick up the box with the number that they have identified and to move around the room collecting that amount of objects. When they have finished their collections, ask them to return to the table with their boxes and check that the correct amount of items has been collected by counting out loud what is inside. When finished, place each box in its correct numerical order with the sandpaper number cards on top.

Support

Younger children can work in pairs helping each other to collect the items.

Extension

Ask older children to find a card to match the one inside the box to the one you point to on the lid.

HOME LINKS
Ask parents and carers to place small collections of items in a bag so that their children can put their hand inside and count how many items are in the bag without looking.

GROUP SIZE
Ten children.

TIMING
20 to 25 minutes.

HOME LINKS
Suggest to parents and carers that while they are out walking with their children they look at house numbers. Copy the photocopiable sheet on page 75 to send home and ask parents and carers to help their children to complete it.

MULTICULTURAL LINKS
Make Divali or Eid cards at the appropriate times of the year and send them to each other.

HERE COMES THE POST

Learning objective

To find out about features of letters and think about letter-writing as an everyday means of communication.

What you need

Display board; ten shoeboxes with lids; paint in different colours; paintbrushes; stick-on labels; small stick-on labels in different shapes; black marker pen; felt-tipped pens; leather satchel; scissors; 1 to 10 number cards (from the 'Plates of numbers' activity on page 25 in Chapter 3); A3 sheet of paper; junk mail and used envelopes; pieces of coloured paper; coloured pencils.

Preparation

Send a letter to parents and carers asking them to bring in any junk mail and used envelopes that they may have at home or work. Cut a hole in the top of each shoebox lid, big enough to put a letter through. Ask each child to paint their shoebox and lid in a colour of their choice.

While the paint is drying, ask each child to put their hand inside the leather satchel and to take out one of the number cards. The number that they have picked will be their box number. Write each child's name and box number on a stick-on label and attach it to the side of their box. Using the A3 sheet of paper, make a list for the display board with each child's box number and name.

What to do

Talk about how the postperson knows where to deliver our letters by looking at the name and address on each envelope. Show the children the chart that you have made with their box numbers displayed and ask them to place their box, in its correct numerical order, on a low table underneath it. Place the junk mail, used envelopes, coloured pencils and so on, on the table, along with the stick-on labels and felt-tipped pens. Invite the children to place stick-on labels over the old addresses on the envelopes and to write new addresses, ensuring that all the numbers are used so that everyone in the group will receive a letter. Provide the small number cards for the children to copy if needed. Ask the children to draw a picture to go inside their letter and to put a stick-on shape 'stamp' on it before placing it in the leather satchel. Let the children take turns being the postperson and to deliver the correct letter to each box number.

Encourage the children to continue the activity over a period of time by 'writing' letters to other children in the group and asking them to check each day if they have any post in their box. Send a letter home to parents and carers explaining what you have been doing and placing these letters in the children's boxes.

Support

Younger children will need help recognizing and writing the numbers so provide number cards that they can trace over.

Extension

Encourage older children to write their own name and number on their box.

This chapter gives ideas that will develop children's ability to move with imagination and control. The games and activities included encourage children to work as teams, navigate obstacle courses, use equipment with control and enjoy moving to various instructions.

Physical development

GROUP SIZE
Ten children.

TIMING
15 to 20 minutes.

HOME LINKS
Ask parents and carers to encourage their children to practise number skills at every available opportunity. For example, count the number of apples in the fruit bowl before and after one has been eaten. Ask questions such as, 'How many will be left if I eat one as well?'.

MULTICULTURAL LINKS

Visit the local music library and borrow a selection of cassettes of music from different nationalities to use to play musical chairs.

MUSICAL CHAIRS

Learning objectives
To move with confidence and in safety; to show awareness of space, of themselves and of others.

What you need
Ten chairs; cassette player; cassette of lively music; a set of 1 to 10 number cards (see the 'Fishing game' activity on page 26 in Chapter 3).

Preparation
Place ten chairs in a line allowing sufficient space for the children to move easily between and around them. Set up a cassette player nearby.

What to do
Ask the children to count out loud how many children there are in the group and how many chairs there are in the row. Ask them to tell you how many girls there are in the group and how many boys. Play the game in the traditional manner by playing a piece of music and asking the children to move in a clockwise direction around the chairs. Emphasize that they must all move in the same direction with no running or pushing.

While the music is playing, remove one of the chairs and place it to one side of the room. When the music stops, the children must all find a chair and sit down. The child who does not have a chair is asked to sit on the chair with the other chairs in the second row. Continue until only one chair and child remain in the main row and all the other children are sitting on chairs in the second one. Ask the children how many chairs are now in the second row and how many remain in the first? Make up a full row of chairs by placing the tenth chair, from the first row, behind the other nine chairs in the second row.

Support
Limit the number of children playing to just five.

Extension
Invite each child to take a card with a number on it. Ask them to tell you which number they are holding and to sit on the chairs in correct numerical order. Start the music and play the game as above. When the game is finished, the children will no longer be sitting in correct numerical order, so ask them to rearrange themselves.

MUSICAL NUMBER PARTNERS

Learning objectives

To move with control and co-ordination; to identify partners by matching number cards and join them on a given signal.

What you need

Coloured marker pens; pieces of coloured card (approximately 10cm x 15cm); pieces of white card (approximately 20cm x 28cm); cassette player and cassette of lively music; stick-on dots; scissors; two shoeboxes; sticky-backed plastic.

Preparation

Make two sets of cards using the pieces of coloured card. Number one of the two sets 1 to 10, ensuring that the same colour pen is used and that all of the numbers are the same size. Make a second set of cards ensuring that each number is written in a different size and colour from that on the first set of cards. On the reverse of each card, attach the corresponding amount of stick-on dots before covering both sets with sticky backed plastic. Using the pieces of white card, make up a set of action cards by drawing a stick figure performing a different action, such as dancing, on each one. Write the word for each action underneath the stick figure and cover with sticky-backed plastic. Decorate two shoeboxes and place both sets of number cards in one box and the action cards in the other.

What to do

Talk to the children about how numbers can be written in many different sizes and colours without their value changing. Show them the set of action cards and make sure that they know what movement each card depicts. Shuffle both sets of number cards and ask each child to take a card from the box before finding a space to stand in around the room. Hold up one of the action cards and ask the children to move in the manner that the card indicates when the music starts playing. When the music stops, each child must find another child who has the same number card as the one they are holding, regardless of the number's shape or colour. Check that they have found the correct matching number card.

Once all of the children have found their partner, they change cards with a child in another pair and continue as before. Before the music starts again, hold up another action card and ask the children to perform that action.

Support

Limit the number of cards to be paired to between one and four, slowly increasing as number recognition skills improve.

Extension

Encourage older children to find their matching number partner by counting the dots on the reverse side of their card and finding another child with the same number of dots.

GROUP SIZE
Four children.

TIMING
15 to 20 minutes.

PEOPLE OF THE WORLD SKITTLES

Learning objective
To handle objects safely and with increasing control.

What you need
Ten identical empty juice bottles with lids; small foam ball; sand; funnel; paint in a variety of colours; paintbrushes; fabric off-cuts and collage materials; glue; spreaders; ten cardboard circles in different skin tone colours; felt-tipped pens; wool in suitable colours for hair; ten stick-on labels; marker pen; A3 sheet of paper; books showing costumes worn by people of different nationalities; the photocopiable sheet on page 59.

Preparation
Wash the bottles thoroughly and then allow to dry before asking the children to help paint them. Leave the paint to dry while the children look in the books at pictures of people in traditional dress. Invite them to decorate the skittles similar to the people in the books using the collage materials. Make faces on the cardboard circles and glue wool on for hair. Remove the lids from each bottle and using the funnel, place a small amount of sand in the bottom of each one. Do not make the bottles too heavy or else they will not fall over when hit by the ball. Glue each bottle's lid in place before attaching a cardboard face to each one. Write number symbols from 1 to 10 on stick-on labels and attach one to the body of each skittle. Using a sheet of A3 paper, make a clearly labelled chart with each child's name, on which to record their scores.

What to do
Place the skittles in an area with enough space for a ball to be thrown without distracting other activities. Place the skittles, suitably spaced, approximately three metres away from a line drawn on the floor to mark where the children must stand when rolling the ball. Encourage the children to take turns rolling the ball to try to knock the skittles down. Ask each child how many skittles they have knocked over and how many are still standing and record their score on the chart.

Alternatively, ask each child to tell you which number skittle they have knocked over by looking at the sticker attached to it. A further extension would be to line the skittles up behind each other before rolling the ball at them. Is it now easier to knock the skittles over than when the skittles were standing next to each other? Let each child continue rolling the ball until they have knocked over all the skittles in the line. How many strikes did it take to knock the whole group of skittles over? Finally, add up the scores. Sing the song, 'Ten little skittles' on the photocopiable sheet on page 59 to complete the activity.

Support
Start with five skittles. Once the children's skills improve, increase the distance between the skittles as well as the number of skittles.

Extension
Line the skittles up in correct numerical order and ask the children to take turns to try to knock over the skittle with the same number as the one you call out. Have someone responsible for replacing a skittle if it is knocked over by mistake.

HOME LINKS
Ask parents and carers, if possible, to take their children to their local bowling alley to play a game and explain how a computer automatically records every player's score on the overhead screen.

GROUP SIZE
Four children.

TIMING
20 minutes.

WALK THE NUMBER LINE

Learning objectives
To move with control and co-ordination; to travel carefully along a specified route.

What you need
Eleven pieces of thick card (approximately 23cm x 23cm); masking tape; marker pen; sticky-backed plastic.

Preparation
Write the numerals 1 to 10 on the pieces of card before covering with sticky-backed plastic. Place the number cards on the floor at equal intervals, making sure that the children will be able to step easily from card to card. Attach the cards securely to the floor with masking tape, in addition to placing a strip of masking tape between each card to show the connection between the numbers.

HOME LINKS
Explain to parents and carers what you have been doing and ask them to play hopscotch at home with their children.

MULTICULTURAL LINKS
Play a hopscotch game from Cuba with the children by drawing seven squares on a concrete area in an arc shape using coloured chalk. Number each section with numerals I to 7 and ask the children to jump or walk from square to square saying the name or counting the number of days in a week as they go.

What to do
Ask the children to remove their shoes and socks. Each of the children should take turns to walk from 0 to 10, counting each card as they step on it. Once they are familiar with walking along the sequence of numbers in this way, ask them to stand on a number card named by you and to move either forwards or backwards according to your instructions. This will help the children to establish a clearer idea of the relationship between the numbers. Keep this very basic by asking them to move either forwards or backwards by just one or two units and then ask them what number they have landed on. Give the other three children a chance to give instructions and to say which number they think the child will land on. Alternatively, ask each child to stand at the beginning of the number line and to jump as far as they can. Again ask them what number they have they landed on.

Support
Make a number line that goes only to six for younger children, and keep any instructions very simple.

Extension
Encourage older children to pretend to be a rocket ship ready for take off by starting at number 10 and counting backwards to 0. Use a set of number cards (see the Plates of numbers activity on page 25 in Chapter 3) and hold them up in random order for the child on the number line to move to that number.

GROUP SIZE
Small groups.

TIMING
25 to 30 minutes.

FOLLOW THE NUMBERS

Learning objective
To travel around, under, over and through balancing and climbing obstacles.

What you need
Suitable items for an obstacle course such as skipping ropes; hula hoops, safety mats, wooden beam; two large cardboard boxes of identical size; chairs; arrows cut from card (approximately 15cm x 25cm); marker pen; masking tape; large area in which to set up; double-sided tape; the photocopiable sheet on page 76; whistle; small circles of yellow card.
NB Constant adult supervision is required for this activity.

Preparation
Make a set of direction arrows numbered from 1 to 10. Make gold medals for each child who takes part by writing '1' on each yellow circle and

attaching a small piece of double-sided tape on the reverse of each. Open both ends of two large cardboard boxes and use masking tape to attach them together to make a tunnel. Set up an obstacle course in a manner that suits your children's abilities, ensuring that there is sufficient space for each child to move safely, securely and freely. The start and finish points should be close to each other and clearly marked using masking tape. Attach the number arrows to the floor with masking tape so that the children do not slip on them. They should also be clearly visible and easy for the children to follow.

What to do
Before starting the activity, walk slowly through the course with the children. Stress that throughout the activity they must move safely and not run. Ask all of the children to stand behind the start line, and when you blow the whistle, the first child starts the course by following the direction of arrow number '1'. Each child must clear each section of the course before the next child starts. Continue the obstacle course until arrow number '10' is reached and the course is complete.

While the children are busy with the course, talk to them about what they are doing. Use terms such as crawl through the boxes, walk around the chairs, walk across the balance beam, throw a beanbag into the bucket, step over a skipping rope and so on. When complete, give each participant a gold medal to wear and ask them which part of the course was their favourite and which was the hardest. Once the children have rested, give them each a copy of the photocopiable sheet on page 76 to complete to consolidate the idea of following a numbered route.

HOME LINKS
Ask parents and carers to arrange a simple numbered obstacle course for their children to do at home.

Support
Limit the amount of obstacles for younger children.

Extension
Place the numbers in random order so that the children have to look for the next number in the sequence.

HENRY HEDGEHOG GAME

Learning objectives
To use small and large equipment; to move with control and co-ordination.

What you need
Four shoeboxes with lids; brown paint; paintbrushes; ten kitchen-roll tubes; scissors; whistle; 20 white stick-on labels; marker pen; glue; spreader; stick-on dots and shapes.

Preparation
Encourage the children to help with making the hedgehogs. Cut the ten kitchen-roll tubes in half equally so that you have 20 lengths, which will be the hedgehogs' spines. Paint the five shoeboxes (hedgehog bodies) and the 20 spines brown. Once dry, give each hedgehog a face using the stick-on dots and shapes. Cut six circular holes in each shoebox lid in which the hedgehog spines can fit. Stick the lid on each shoebox ensuring that they are firmly attached. Attach a 1 to 5 number label to each set of five spines. Designate an area to be the start and finish line and another area where the hedgehogs will be placed.

What to do
Divide the children into four groups of five and explain the game to them. Give each child in each group a numbered hedgehog spine. When the whistle blows, the first child in each group must run to the hedgehog shape and fit the spine that they are holding into its body before returning to their group. Once they have crossed the line, the next child in the group takes a turn. The last child in each group to place the spine in the hedgehog's body must pick up the whole hedgehog and return with it to their place in the line. The group who are all sitting down and have a complete hedgehog are the winners. Ask each group of children to tell you how many spines Henry Hedgehog has in his body.

Support
Limit the number of groups of children from four to just two.

Extension
Attach a set of small stick-on labels numbered 1 to 5 on each hedgehog. Hand out the spines to each child in random order and ask them to place the spines in their correct position in each hedgehog's body by matching the number on the hedgehog to the number on the spine that they are holding.

GROUP SIZE
Four children.

TIMING
15 to 20 minutes.

CROQUET

Learning objectives
To handle tools and objects safely and with increasing control; to move with co-ordination.

What you need
Ten shoeboxes without lids; paint in a variety of colours; paintbrushes; ten large stick-on labels; marker pen; coloured stick-on dots; eight kitchen-roll tubes; masking tape; a foam ball.

Preparation
Make a set of croquet tunnels by cutting big archways in the long sides of each shoebox. Ensure that the holes are big enough for the ball to go through with ease. Attach the kitchen-roll tubes together in twos using masking tape to make four mallets. Paint the mallets and ten shoeboxes in bright colours. Number all the stick-on labels with numerals 1 to 10 before attaching the corresponding amount of coloured dots alongside each number. Once the paint on the shoeboxes has dried, stick one label to each box on the flat surface on the top. Continue until all ten shoeboxes have been clearly labelled.

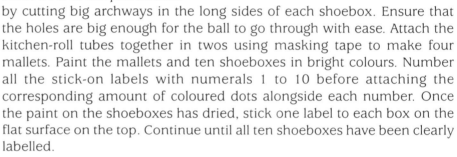

What to do
Arrange the shoeboxes in random number order in a large open area allowing sufficient space for the children to move easily between them. Explain to the children that the game of croquet is very old and has been played by people throughout the world for a long time. Keep the rules very simple so that the children are not distracted from finding the next number in its correct sequence. Show the children how to hit the ball lightly with the mallet so that it will go through each archway following the correct numerical order. Explain that if after hitting the ball, it does not go through the correct archway, then the next child takes a turn.

Once the children have successfully passed each number, they can move on to the next one. While the children are playing, ask them to tell you which number will be the next one they have to hit the ball through, which number they have just passed, which number will come next and so on. Continue until all ten archways have been passed.

Support
Limit the number of archways to just five ensuring that they are placed in their correct numerical order.

Extension
Cover the numbers with small pieces of paper and ask the children to find the next number in the correct numerical order by counting the number of dots on each archway. The children could repeat the course by playing backwards, working from number '10' to number '1'.

HOME LINKS
Invite parents and carers to take the croquet set home overnight to play with their children or to play a shop-bought version together.

NUMBER RELAY

Learning objectives
To work as a team to follow directions; to move with confidence and in safety.

What you need
Twenty eight pieces of thick coloured card (measuring approximately 15cm x 15cm); stick-on shapes of different objects; sticky-backed plastic; scissors, marker pen; the photocopiable sheet on page 77; small box; envelope; whistle.

Preparation
Make two identical sets of 1 to 6 number cards on 12 of the pieces of card. On the other 14 pieces of card, make two sets of cards by sticking on collections of sticky shapes such as one star, two bells and so on, in groups of one to six. You will have an extra set of two cards, the reason for this will become obvious once you start playing. Cover both sets of cards with sticky-backed plastic. Shuffle the two sets of picture cards and place in a small box and store the two sets of number cards in an envelope.

What to do
Place the box with the picture cards in the centre of a room on a table. Divide the children into two groups of six and ask them to stand in a line behind a marked area, ensuring that both groups are the same distance away from the box. Give each child a card with a number written on it making sure that both groups have a full set of numbers from 1 to 6. Explain that when you blow the whistle, the first child in each group must run to the box and find the card in the box with the number of pictures on it that corresponds with their number card. Once they have found the matching card, they must take it out of the box and return to their group while the next child takes a turn. The group that finishes first, with everyone sitting quietly on the floor wins the game.

When both groups are finished, ask the children to rearrange themselves so that they are standing in correct numerical order. Check to see if they have all collected the correct matching picture card. The reason for having the extra two sets of picture cards is that when the last child in each group takes their turn, they will also have a choice of cards and will have to think about which card to choose.

Give each child a copy of the photocopiable sheet on page 77 for them to complete.

Support
Help younger children to identify the number on their card before the start of the game.

Extension
When the game is complete, invite older children to sort both sets of cards in their correct numerical order making one-to-one correspondence, by placing one set underneath the other.

CHAPTER 6

This chapter inspires children's mathematical learning through a range of creative activities. Numbers are explored through filling in nature charts, making number necklaces and playing a water xylophone, among many other inventive ideas.

Creative development

GROUP SIZE
Whole group.

TIMING
25 to 30 minutes for a walk; 20 to 25 minutes for the collage.

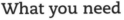

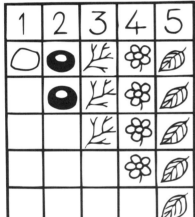

HOME LINKS
Copy the photocopiable sheet on page 78 for parents and carers and ask them to help their child complete it at home.

NATURE COLLAGE

Learning objectives
To explore natural colour, texture and shape in two and three dimensions; to respond in a variety of ways to what they see and touch.

What you need
A3 sheets of paper; sticky tape; pieces of green card; thick glue; spreaders; marker pen.

Preparation
Visit a nature area in advance and make a number chart showing pictures of suitable items. Copy the chart onto A3 sheets of paper, before folding each one in half and joining the sides with sticky tape. Leave the top section open to form a folder. Print each child's name clearly in the top left-hand corner of their folder, encouraging older children to write their own names. Organize extra adult helpers to accompany you on your walk.

What to do
Give each child their folder and explain that you are all going to go on a walk and collect interesting natural things to make a class collage. Emphasize the importance of collecting items off the ground and discourage the children from picking leaves and flowers that are still growing. During the walk, talk to the children about how many of each item they need to collect and what they see. Once all the collections are complete, return to your setting and arrange the art material on the table. Ask the children to choose a piece of card on which to mount their collection. Stress that they can arrange the items in any order and position they wish. When all the collages are complete, allow the glue to dry thoroughly before displaying the finished work.

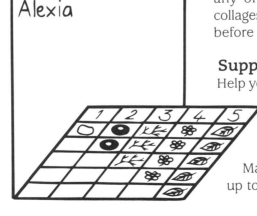

Support
Help younger children to identify the correct amount of items required, starting with collections of just three.

Extension
Make a chart that requires the children to collect up to ten different items.

GROUP SIZE
Five children.

TIMING
20 to 25 minutes.

PUFFY PAINT NUMBER PICTURES

Learning objectives
To make three-dimensional number pictures; to create number patterns using a widening range of materials.

What you need
Five A3 sheets of coloured card; black marker pen; coloured pencils; glue; spreaders; plastic squeeze bottles; sticky labels; coloured dots; marker pen; containers for collage materials; selection of large collage materials such as buttons, pasta shapes, pieces of fabric, beads; the photocopiable sheet on page 79; puffy paint ingredients.

Preparation
Place different batches of previously made coloured puffy paint into each squeeze bottle. Make a colour label for each bottle by placing a sticky coloured dot of the same colour on each bottle. On each sheet of A3 card, draw a large number in the centre using a black marker pen starting with number '1' on the first piece through to number '5'. Draw large circles around each number. Repeat this process depending on the number of children in your group. Ensure that you have doubles of each number for each group to avoid conflict as some children will want the same number as their friend. Sort the collage materials into different containers and place these along with the glue, spreaders and coloured pencils in the centre of the table.

What to do
Invite each child to choose one of the pieces of card with a number written on it. Ask them to say which number they have chosen and then to colour in the number using the coloured pencils. Explain that using the collage materials, they must fill each circle surrounding the number on their card with the corresponding amount of objects. For example, in the circles surrounding the number '5', place five buttons in one circle, five pieces of fabric in another and so on. When this section of the activity is complete, place the puffy paint on the table so that the children can start building up their number pictures. Show them how to squeeze the paint out and encourage them to paint around the outline of the number on their card and circles. They can also make lines joining the number to the different circles. Allow the paint and glue to dry thoroughly before asking the children to place their pictures in the correct numerical order on a display board. Please bear in mind that if two children in the same group have chosen the same number, then the second picture with the same number must be placed underneath the first picture, in order that the number sequence is not broken. When this happens, ask the children what other numbers are missing from that number sequence.

HOME LINKS
Make a pendant for a family member using a plastic lid covered with a puffy paint design.

Support
Reduce the numbers from five to three for younger children.

Extension
Encourage each child to make a mount for their painting by sticking it onto a larger piece of thick card.

NUMBER NECKLACES

Learning objectives
To explore colour, texture and form in three dimensions; to create a pattern following a number sequence.

What you need
Coloured bootlaces; drinking straws; scissors; sticky tape; small squares of card labelled 1 to 5 (one set per child); skewers; the photocopiable sheet on page 79; play dough ingredients; greased baking tray; wire rack; containers; paint; paintbrushes; sticky labels; marker pen.

Preparation
Make a batch of play dough the day before you do the activity, encouraging the children to help. Give a set of small 1 to 5 number cards to each child in the group. Cut drinking straws into small pieces and attach these to the back of each number card with a piece of sticky tape. Place each set of number cards in a separate container labelled with each child's name. Knot each bootlace at one end so that the beads will not fall off during threading. Allow at least two days to complete the activity so that there is time for the play dough beads to harden in an oven in addition to the paint drying.

What to do
Give each child a ball of play dough and ask them to mould a number of beads from the dough. When the beads have been modelled, make holes in each one by pushing them onto a skewer. (**NB** The skewers are not for use by the children and must be kept well out of reach.) Place the skewers on a greased baking tray and cook at a low temperature of approximately 100°C (225°F or Gas Mark 2) for between six to eight hours, or until the beads are hard. Leave the skewers in place during the cooking process so that the holes do not close. Remove the baking tray from the oven making sure that the children are out of the way as the beads and skewers will be hot. Place the beads on a wire rack to cool before removing the skewers.

When the beads are cool enough, encourage the children to paint their beads in colours of their choice. Once the paint has dried, each child must place their set of beads in their named container. Give each child an additional container with the number cards inside as well as a coloured bootlace. Invite each child to find the number 1 card and to take it out of the container and thread the bootlace through the straw on the back. Ask them to thread the equivalent amount of beads onto the bootlace following each number card; so that they would have one bead following card number 1, two beads after card number 2 and so on. Ask the children questions as they work as to what number card will follow the one that they have just threaded. Continue until all the number cards have been threaded with the corresponding amount of cards and beads in their correct numerical order. Finally, knot the two ends of the necklace together.

Support
Younger children can make necklaces with fewer beads and may need help identifying the correct number cards in the container.

Extension
Let older children make number cards to 10 to use on longer necklaces.

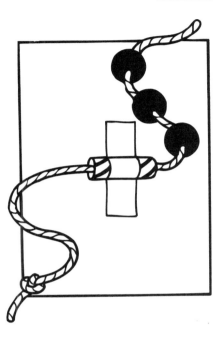

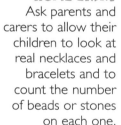

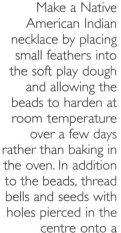

GROUP SIZE
Small groups.

TIMING
20 minutes.

WATER XYLOPHONE

Learning objectives

To express and communicate their ideas by using a variety of songs and musical instruments; to recognize and explore how sounds can be changed.

What you need

Eight glass milk bottles; sticky labels; marker pen; food colouring; funnel; measuring jug; dowelling stick; cork; metal spoon; fork; twigs; pencil, shallow box; the photocopiable sheet on page 60; a piece of card.

Preparation

Write the numbers 1 to 8 on eight sticky labels, and stick one label onto each of the eight milk bottles. Pour a small amount of water into a measuring jug and add a few drops of food colouring. Using a funnel, pour this water into the bottle numbered 1 up to a few centimetres from the top. Repeat this process, changing the colour of the water each time and gradually decreasing the water levels in each bottle. It is a good idea to hit each bottle gently with a spoon to see if they are in tone. Attach a piece of cork to the end of a piece of dowelling rod to make a striking stick and place all the other striking sticks, spoon, fork and so on, into a shallow box. Place the bottles in their correct numerical order on a low table alongside the striking sticks. Copy the number music and words for the song 'Two Little Dicky Birds' (Traditional) on the photocopiable sheet on page 60, and mount it on a piece of card. Ensure that you will be able to provide close adult supervision throughout the activity.

What to do

Let children take turns 'playing' the water xylophone by gently tapping each bottle with the different striking sticks and observing the difference in tone between the bottles. Ask them to talk about the sounds that they hear and point to the bottle that makes the lowest or highest tone. Explain that the bottle numbered 1 makes the lowest tone as it has the most water in it, whereas the bottle numbered 8 makes the highest tone as it has the least water in it. Rearrange the bottles and ask the children to place them back in their correct numerical order. Teach the children the song, 'Two Little Dicky Birds' and ask them to take turns tapping out the tune on the water xylophone by following the simple number music.

Encourage the children to experiment with the tone by increasing the water levels in each bottle. Once the bottles have been emptied, let the children gently tap each bottle again in order to observe that each bottle now sounds identical.

Support

Limit the number of bottles to just three and encourage the children to experiment freely with the bottles using the various striking sticks and noting their difference in tone.

Extension

Older children will enjoy following the number music and the other children should be encouraged to sing along to the water xylophone accompaniment. Encourage the children to experiment with making up their own tunes on the bottles.

HOME LINKS
Ask parents and carers to supervise their children at home in experimenting with using drinking glasses instead of milk bottles and a variety of different striking sticks.

GROUP SIZE
Two to three
children.

TIMING
20 to 25 minutes.

STEPHIE'S WEB

Learning objective
To respond to patterns in nature and recreate them following a number sequence.

What you need
Thick pieces of blue rectangular card; hole-punch; marker pen; bodkins; thick, white glittery wool; scissors; black pipe-cleaners; black construction paper; sticky tape; glue; spreaders; dot stickers.

Preparation
Punch ten holes around the edge of each piece of card and write the numbers 1 to 10 under each hole, out of sequence. Thread the bodkins with white wool and tie a knot at one end. Place all the materials required for the activity in the centre of a low table.

What to do
Talk to the children about spiders and how they spin silk threads to make their webs. Ask if any of the children have seen a spider's web and if so, what they thought of it. Give each child a card and a threaded bodkin; older children should be encouraged to thread their own. Invite them to make a spider's web, starting at number 1 and finishing at number 10. Attach the knotted end of each child's piece of wool firmly with sticky tape underneath number 1. Stress the importance of sewing the web by following the numbers in their correct order. When the sewing is complete, cut the excess wool off and secure the end underneath number 10 at the back.

To complete the web, ask each child to cut a spider shape from black construction paper. Glue four pipe-cleaners to the bottom side of each spider to give it eight bendy legs and stick on two dot stickers for eyes. Once the glue has dried, slip 'Stephie' into her web, bending her legs so that they stick up inside the web and hold her in place.

Support
Use the numbers 1 to 6 only, drawing lines between the numbers for younger children to follow to ensure that the correct number sequence is followed.

Extension
Encourage older children to help make and number their own web.

HOME LINKS
Ask parents and carers to take time to look for spiders' webs with their children first thing in the morning when they are covered in dew.

GROUP SIZE
Two to three
children.

TIMING
20 minutes.

COLOURFUL MOSAICS

Learning objectives
To experiment with different materials to make a picture; to explore colour and texture in two dimensions.

What you need:
Large sheets of A3 coloured card; buttons; crushed eggshells; gummed shapes; foil balls; tissue balls; painted pasta shapes and four other suitable collage materials; paint in a variety of colours; paintbrushes; five clean margarine containers; five pieces of card; thick glue; spreaders; rolling pin; scissors; coloured pencils; the photocopiable sheet on page 80; sticky labels; marker pen.

Preparation
Write the numbers 1 to 5 on a set of five sticky labels and attach to the five thoroughly washed margarine containers. Divide the containers in half by anchoring a piece of card inside each one. Wash and dry some eggshells thoroughly and place in a warm oven to dry. Ask the children to help paint the eggshells and when the paint is dry, place them in a plastic bag and crush them with a rolling pin. Place the eggshells in one side of the container marked number 1 and place buttons in the second side. Fill the remaining four containers with suitable collage materials. Copy the flower on the photocopiable sheet on page 80 onto A3 sheets of card, one for each child. Place the collage materials on a low table making sure that the containers are in their correct numerical order.

What to do
Invite the children to colour in their flower picture using the coloured pencils. Once complete, explain that they must look at their picture carefully and find the section numbered 1. They must then look for the container marked number 1 as only collage materials in this container must be used for that portion of the picture. Emphasize that they can use collage materials from either section of each container providing them with more choice. Continue in this manner until all five sections of the picture have been filled with the correct collage materials. Invite the children to use the collage materials as they wish around the flower to individualize their picture.

Support
Reduce the number of sections of the picture to between just one and three.

Extension
Ask older children to draw their own pictures, dividing them up and numbering the different sections.

HOME LINKS
Send a letter home to parents and carers telling them what scrap materials you require for this activity and asking them to start collecting.

GROUP SIZE
Whole group.

TIMING
25 to 30 minutes.

FINGER PUPPET FUN

Learning objective
To express and communicate their ideas using a widening range of materials, imagination, role-play and songs.

What you need
Small strips of white rectangular cardboard; scraps of white fabric and wool; glue; spreaders; felt-tipped pens; coloured dot stickers; shoebox for the storage of the finger puppets; small white paper circles; containers for the collage materials; sticky tape; scissors; 'Five Little Ducks' from *This Little Puffin...* compiled by Elizabeth Matterson (Puffin Books).

Preparation
Cut strips of white card long enough to fit around a child's middle finger. Place all the collage materials in suitable containers on a table.

What to do
Invite each child to make a duck finger puppet using the materials provided. Fit each piece of card individually to each child's finger by winding it round their middle finger and sticking the two ends together with sticky tape. Draw a beak on each circle and give it coloured dots for eyes and fabric scraps for feathers. Each puppet should be clearly numbered from 1 to 5. Stick the decorated ducks onto the cardboard rings. Once the glue has dried, sit with the children and sing the number rhyme 'Five Little Ducks'.

Place five of the finger puppets made by the children on your own hand, in their correct numerical order, to show the children how to act out the rhyme. During the course of the rhyme, ask the children how many ducks will be left after the first little duck disappears – some children will be able to identify the amount left on your fingers just by looking. At the end of the rhyme, put all of the puppets back on your fingers and ask how many there are. Let the children take turns to place the five finger puppets on their fingers while the other children sing the rhyme.

HOME LINKS
Encourage parents and carers to sing other finger rhymes or songs involving numbers with their children.

MULTICULTURAL LINKS
Talk to the children about the Jewish Festival of Light, which is called Hanukkah. Make eight little candle finger puppets.

Support
Teach the children the rhyme, 'Five Little Ducks' well in advance of the activity. Encourage them to remove a puppet from their finger one at a time, as they sing, as bending a finger down is not always easy for them.

Extension
Make additional sets of finger puppets for the children to use. Teach them number rhymes up to ten, such as 'Ten Green Bottles' from *This Little Puffin...* compiled by Elizabeth Matterson (Puffin Books).

GROUP SIZE
Six children.

TIMING
20 to 25 minutes.

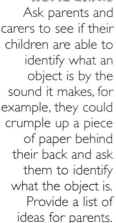

HOME LINKS
Ask parents and carers to see if their children are able to identify what an object is by the sound it makes, for example, they could crumple up a piece of paper behind their back and ask them to identify what the object is. Provide a list of ideas for parents.

SHAKE AND RATTLE

Learning objective
To recognize repeated sounds and respond to them in a variety of ways.

What you need
Buttons; stones; beads; pasta shapes; coloured pencils; scissors; 12 yoghurt pots and 12 clear plastic cups; sticky tape; paint in one colour; paintbrushes; sticky labels; coloured dots; containers; number cards 1 to 6 (see the 'Plates of numbers' activity on page 25 in Chapter 3); two shoeboxes; a marker pen.

Preparation
Collect 12 identical yoghurt pots, wash them thoroughly and with the children's help, paint them all the same colour so that the children will have to identify the shakers by sound rather than how they look. Leave the 12 plastic cups as they are. Once the paint on the pots is dry, place one coloured pencil in the bottom of one of the pots and one in the bottom of one of the clear plastic cups. Place two buttons in the second yoghurt pot and cup, three beads in the following two and so on, until all 12 have been filled. Vary the contents in the shakers according to what materials you have at your disposal. Attach a spare yoghurt pot firmly to each filled yoghurt pot with sticky tape, and do the same with plastic cups to make two different sets of shakers: one transparent, one not. On the bottom of the first set of shakers containing one object, write number 1 and stick on one dot. On the second set, write number 2 and stick on two dots and so on until all the shakers are labelled with numbers to 6.

What to do
Place the shakers on a table and encourage the children to take turns shaking them and listening to the different sounds that they make. Place the 1 to 6 number cards on a low table with the transparent shakers in one box and the yoghurt pot shakers in another. Give each of the six children one of the yoghurt pot shakers from the box and remove one of the transparent sound shakers from the other box. Ask the children how many items are in the shaker that you are holding. Shake the shaker a few times asking the children to listen carefully to the sound it makes and encouraging them to describe it. Invite each child to take a turn to shake the shaker that they are holding and ask them to identify by sound who is holding the matching partner of the shaker you have.

When the children think that they have identified the correct shaker, see if they are right by turning the shaker over and checking what number is written underneath. If it is correct, ask the child with that shaker to place it in its correct position on the number line. The shaker that you are holding should be placed with its pair. Continue in this manner until all the shakers are in their correct position on the number line.

Support
Colour code the shakers with stickers to aid the identification of pairs.

Extension
Introduce simple rhythmic patterns to the children by shaking out a simple pattern such as one shake, two shakes, one shake and so on, which the children must listen to and then repeat using the other shakers.

The birthday party

It was Luigi's fourth birthday today and he was having
a big birthday party. Luigi's grandma, aunts and
uncles were coming, as well as four of his playgroup
friends. Mum had made jellies, cakes, sandwiches and
crispy pavlovas (meringues) filled with fruit and cream.

'Where's my birthday cake?' Luigi asked, excitedly.

'You can't see it yet,' said Mum. 'Now, let's lay the
table. Everyone will be here soon.' Luigi and his four
friends were sitting around the table to eat.

'I'll put out the plates and you put out the dishes,'
said Mum, giving Luigi some paper dishes.

Mum put a plate by each chair. 'One, two, three, four, five!' she counted. 'Just
enough!'

Luigi put a dish by each chair. 'One, two, three, four… oh dear,' he sighed.

'You've got two stuck together,' smiled Mum, pulling the dishes apart.

'*Now* can I see my birthday cake?' asked Luigi.

'Not yet,' said Mum. 'We have to put out the cups and spoons.'

Mum put a cup by each plate. 'One, two, three, four, five!' she counted. Just
enough!'

Luigi put a spoon by each dish. 'One, two, three, four… oh dear,' he sighed.

'You need another one!' smiled Mum, passing it to him.

'*Now* can I see my birthday cake?' asked Luigi.

'Not yet,' said Mum. 'We have to give everyone a party hat and blower.'

Mum put out the party hats. 'One, two, three, four, five!' she counted. 'Just
enough!'

Luigi put out the blowers. 'One, two, three, four… oh dear,' he sighed.

'You've dropped one on the floor,' Mum told him, picking it up.

Just then, the doorbell rang. 'Time for the party to start,' said Mum, going to
answer the door.

'Happy birthday!' shouted Luigi's grandma, aunts and friends as they all piled
into the house. Luigi had so many cards and presents he couldn't count them all!

'*Now* can I see my birthday cake?' he asked, when he'd opened all his presents.

'Of course you can,' said Mum, going to fetch it.

She returned, carrying a huge, scrumptious-looking chocolate cake decorated
with white icing. On the top were four lighted candles. Everyone gasped.

'Blow out the candles, Luigi!' everyone shouted.

Luigi counted the candles.

'One, two, three, four… just enough!' he shouted.
And he blew them all out with one big puff.

© Karen King

At the supermarket

Bottles and boxes,
Packets and cans,
So many shelves
For the stackers to fill.
Cartons and canisters,
Parcels and jars,
So many items
To ring through the till.

Dad chooses butter, Mum prefers marge,
I pick a packet of tea-bags marked 'large'.
A big label tells us some things are reduced,
So into our trolley go four packs of juice.

Mother and fathers,
Uncles and aunts,
So many shoppers
With trolleys to fill.
Wallets and purses,
Cheque books and cards,
So many pennies
To pay at the till.

Grandpa takes grapes and apples for Gran,
Mum can't find milk so she asks for a man,
'Milk is with eggs on the shelf at the back,'
Says the man who is helping a lady to pack.

Bottles and boxes,
Packets and cans,
So many shelves
For the stackers to fill.
Cartons and canisters,
Parcels and jars,
So many items
To ring through the till

© Celia Warren

Ten little skittles
(Tune: 'Ten Green Bottles') (Traditional)

1. Ten lit - tle skit - tles_ stand - ing in a row. Ten lit - tle skit - tles_ stand - ing in a row. If you

knock one down there will still be nine to go, Yes nine lit - tle skit - tles_ stand - ing in a row.

Verse 2 Nine green skittles...
Verse 3 Eight green skittles...
and so on

Words: Ann Bryant

Two little dicky birds

Two little dicky birds sitting on a wall,
One named Peter, one named Paul,
Fly away Peter, fly away Paul,
Come back Peter, come back Paul.

Traditional

Pinkie pig game game

Multicultural people game

Fruit bowl

Fill the bowl with fruit.

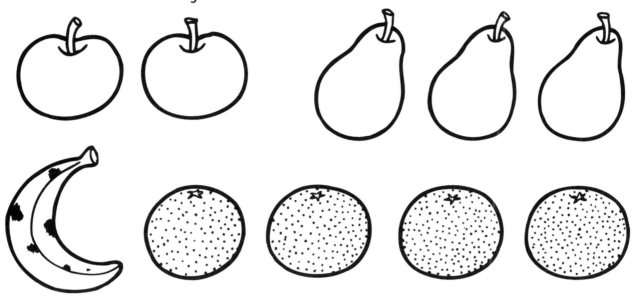

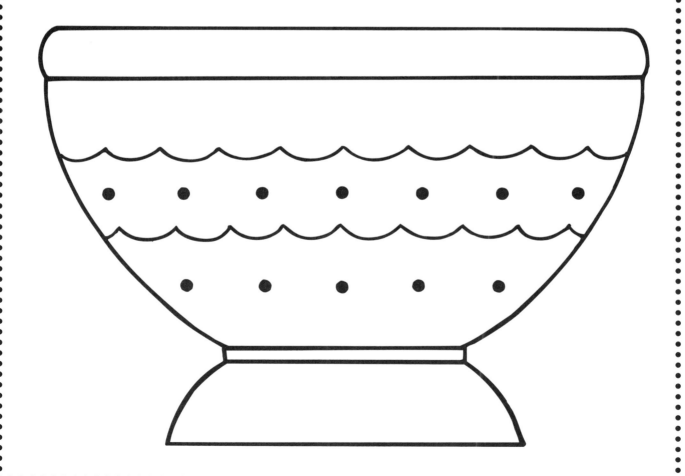

Recipe for barfi

What you need

- ■ wooden spoon
- ■ large saucepan
- ■ 2 shallow rectangular-shaped trays
- ■ 100g (4oz) desiccated coconut
- ■ 75g (3oz) sugar
- ■ 1 litre (2 pints) milk
- ■ 2 crushed cardamom seeds
- ■ Pink food colouring

Method

- ■ Grease the two rectangular-shaped trays.
- ■ Place the milk in a saucepan and heat over a high temperature until it starts to boil.
- ■ Turn down the temperature and allow the milk to simmer until it is reduced to about half a litre.
- ■ Stir in the sugar, cardamom seeds and coconut and continue cooking until the mixture thickens, stirring all the time.
- ■ Pour half of the mixture into one of the greased dishes.
- ■ Add a few drops of pink food colouring to the remaining mixture and stir well.
- ■ Place the remainder of mixture into the second greased dish and leave both to set.
- ■ When cool, and set, cut the sweet into small squares for the children to try.

Telephone call

Fill in the missing numbers and colour in the telephone.

Let's play dominoes

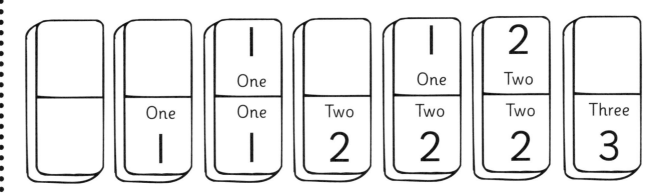
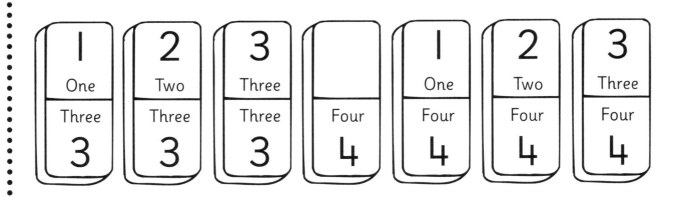
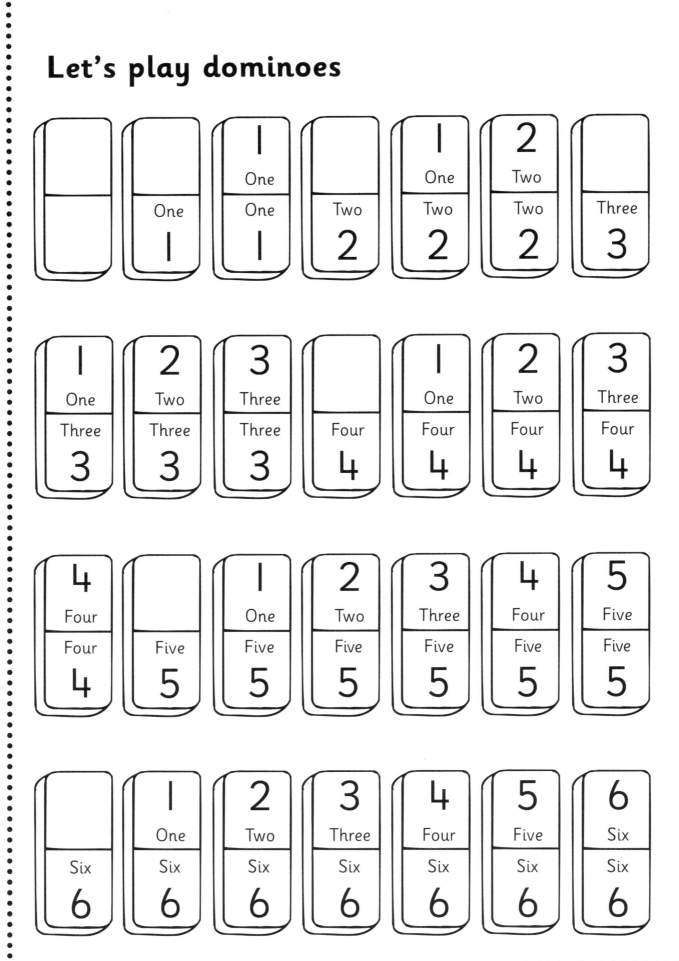
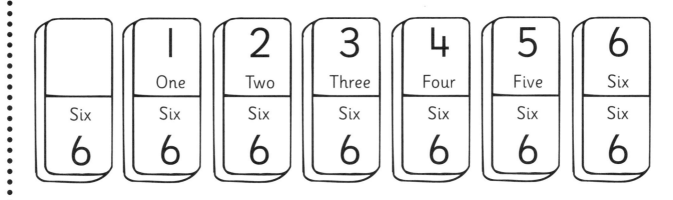

Rugby numbers

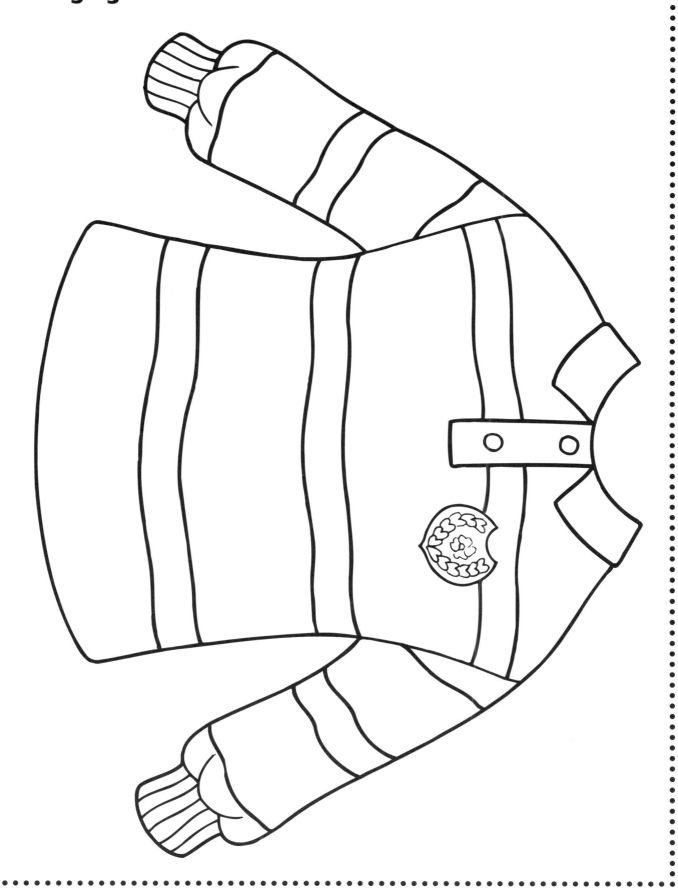

Speech pattern

♩ = 1 clap   ⊔ = 2 claps

Adult
Say and clap hands:

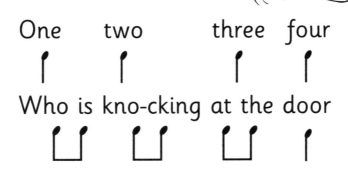

| One | two | three | four |
| ♩ | ♩ | ♩ | ♩ |

Who is kno-cking at the door
⊔   ⊔   ⊔   ♩

Children
Say and clap hands:

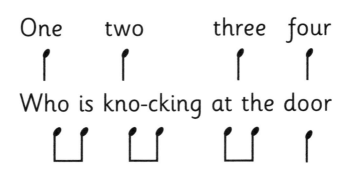

| One | two | three | four |
| ♩ | ♩ | ♩ | ♩ |

Who is kno-cking at the door
⊔   ⊔   ⊔   ♩

Adult
Say and stamp feet:

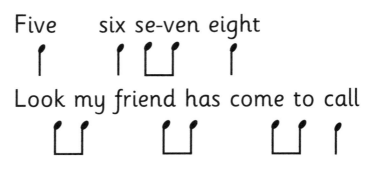

Five   six se-ven eight
♩   ♩ ⊔   ♩

Look my friend has come to call
⊔   ⊔   ⊔   ♩

Children
Say and stamp feet:

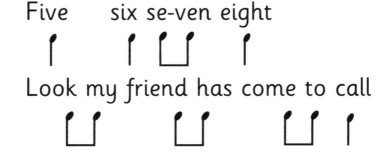

Five   six se-ven eight
♩   ♩ ⊔   ♩

Look my friend has come to call
⊔   ⊔   ⊔   ♩

Froggies on a wall

Float and sink experiment

Step 1
Pour water into bowl.

Step 2
Place bottle without lid on in water. 'What happens?'

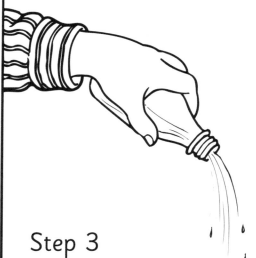

Step 3
Empty water out of bottle. Screw on bottle's lid.

Step 4
Place bottle with lid on in water. 'What happens?'

Join the dots

Complete the next picture in each line.
Count how many there are and write the number in the box.

Ten little fishes

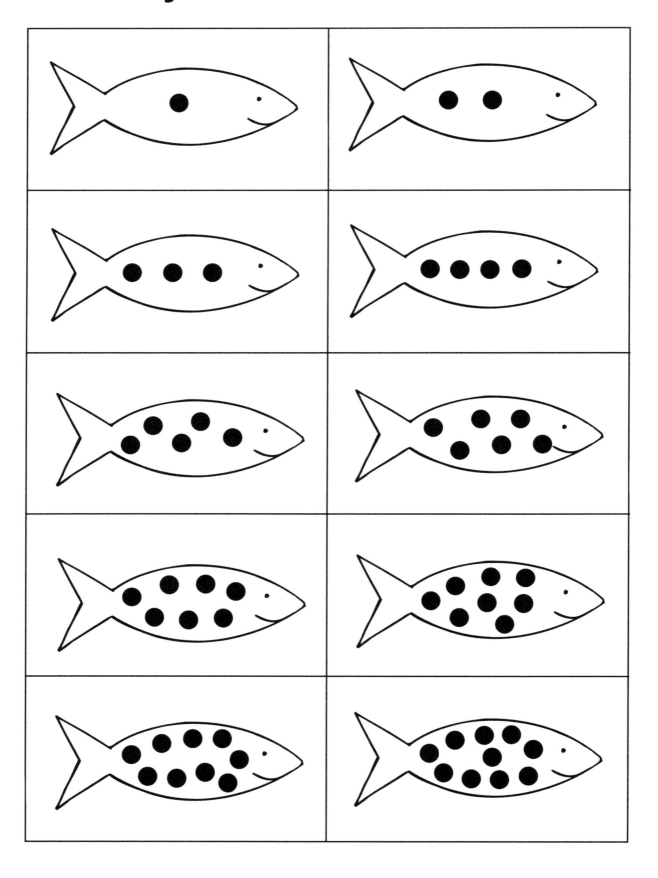

How many sweets?

Guess how many sweets are in the jar.
Look for each number and colour each sweet the same.

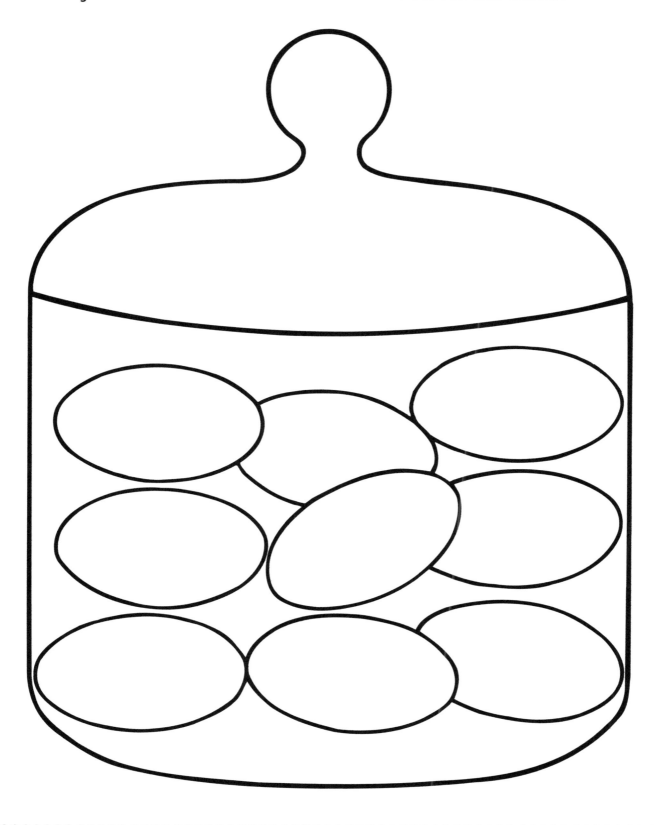

Arabic numbers

1 ١	2 ٢	3 ٣	4 ٤
5 ٥	6 ٦	7 ٧	8 ٨
9 ٩	10 ١٠	11 ١١	12 ١٢
13 ١٣	14 ١٤	15 ١٥	16 ١٦
17 ١٧	18 ١٨	19 ١٩	20 ٢٠

Deliver the mail

Help to deliver the mail by filling in the missing house numbers.

Draw a line connecting the letters to the correct houses.

Number to number

Join the numbers from 1 to 10.

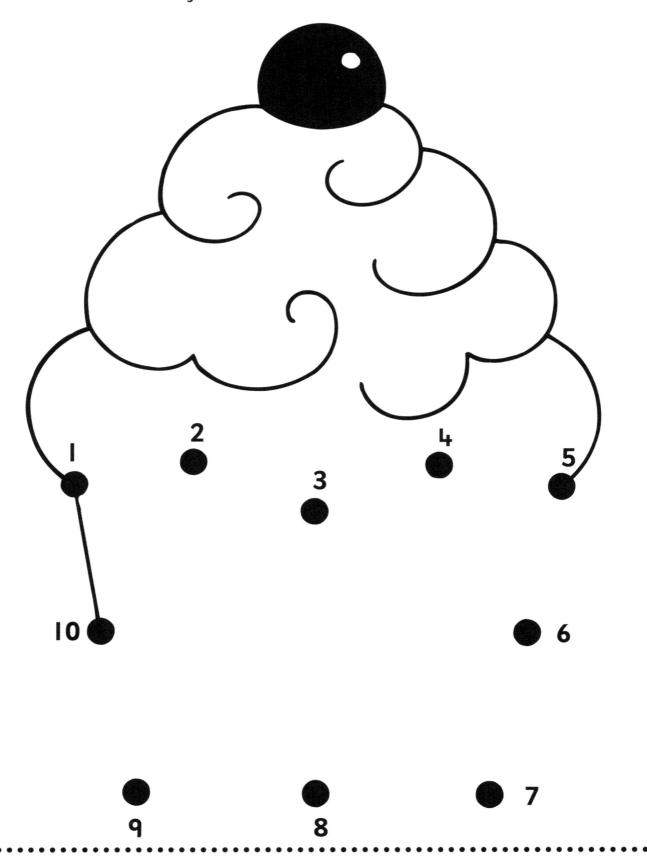

Number match

Draw lines to match the pictures to the correct numbers.
Colour the pictures.

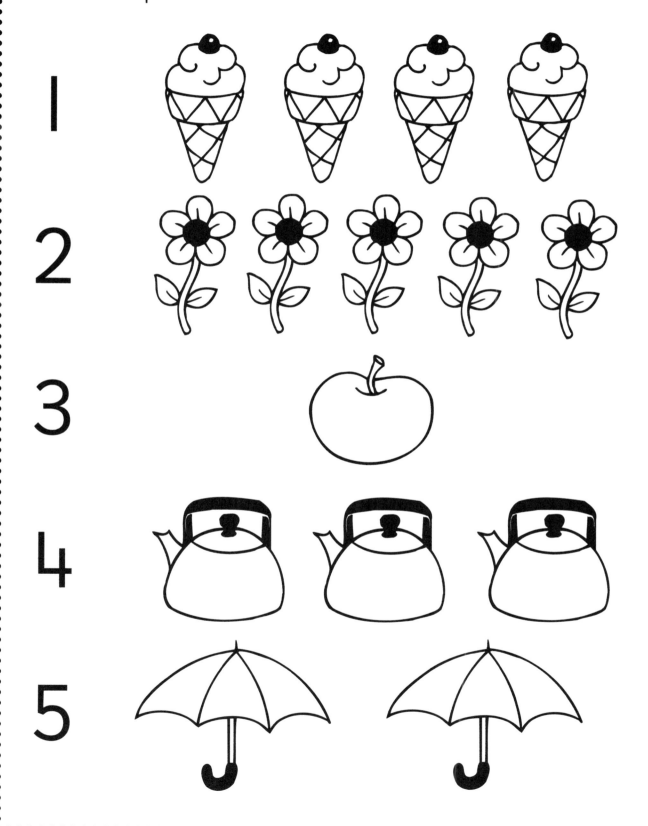

1

2

3

4

5

Make a collection

Look for the correct number of items.

1	2	3	4	5
🍵				
📖	📖			
🧦	🧦	🧦		
🥄	🥄	🥄	🥄	
🧸	🧸	🧸	🧸	🧸

Puffy paint

What you need

Large mixing bowl; wooden spoon; measuring cup; flour; salt; water; food colouring in a variety of colours; several shallow bowls.

Method

■ Mix equal parts of flour and salt together with small amounts of water.

■ Continue adding water until the texture is that of soft dough.

■ Place small amounts of this dough into the shallow bowls adding a different food colouring to each one.

Playdough recipe

Double quantities depending on the amount needed.

What you need

2 cups flour; 1 cup salt; ½ cup water; 2tbsp oil; large mixing bowl; jug; measuring cup; wooden spoon; baking board; airtight container.

Method

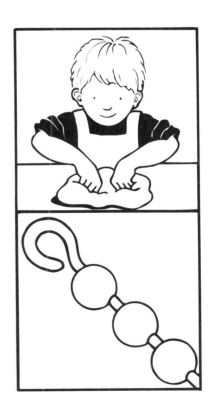

■ Mix the flour and salt together in a large mixing bowl.

■ Add the oil to the dry mixture.

■ Gradually add the water to the mixture stirring at first with a wooden spoon and then kneading the mixture with your hands until you have a smooth lump of dough. Add more water if the dough is too stiff or more flour if too sticky.

■ Knead the dough on a baking board coated with flour before placing in an airtight container in the fridge until needed.

Once modelled, the above dough can be dried in a warm oven or left to dry at room temperature for a couple of days.

Flower mosaic

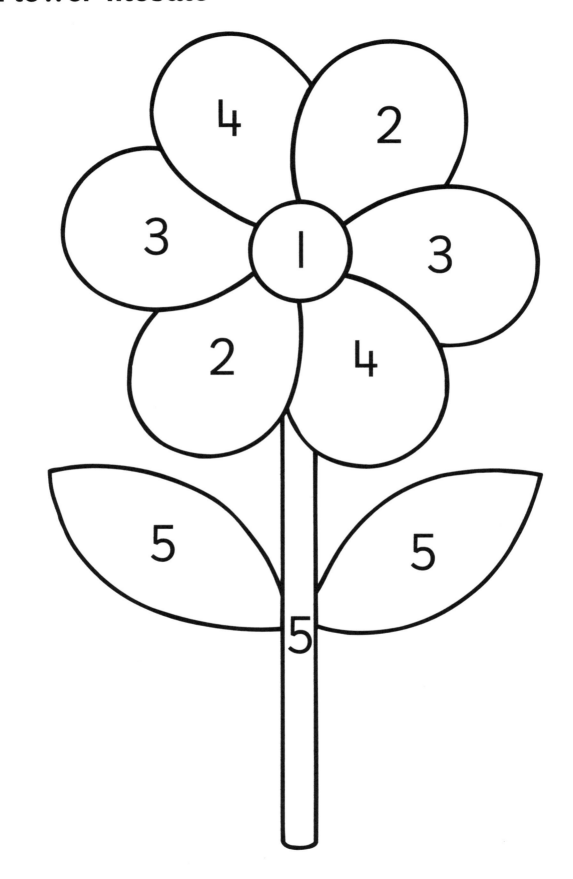